# ELLEV8

## BOOK ONE
## LETTING THE LIGHT IN

KAREN KENNABY

WWW.ELLEV8.WORLD

Copyright © 2025 Karen Kennaby
All Rights Reserved.

# CONTENTS

| | |
|---|---|
| Invitation | 1 |
| Acknowledgments | 4 |
| Executive Summary | 6 |
| Chapter 1: Starting with the Basics | 9 |
| Chapter 2: Phases of Life | 25 |
| Chapter 3: We're All Broken, and We're Also All Whole | 39 |
| Chapter 4: Hearing Where You Are | 55 |
| Chapter 5: Speaking Your Truth | 77 |
| Chapter 6: Seeing Clearly | 101 |
| Chapter 7: Rising Above | 123 |
| Chapter 8: Integration | 145 |
| Next Steps for the Reader | 163 |

# INVITATION

**Dear Ellev8'ing One,**

Every morning when I open my window to greet the day, I'm reminded of something profound: transformation isn't about becoming someone new - it's about letting the light illuminate who we've always been.

This book is born from years, decades in fact, of walking alongside people as they discover their own light. It's about the moments when something shifts inside us, when we feel ourselves standing taller, breathing deeper, trusting more fully in who we are.

Ellev8 comes out of my purpose and my mission to help more women really shine their light. I'm on a mission to inspire 100,000 women to shine their light by 2035 and this is all about really shining the light both internally and externally so we finally overcome the darkness. Everything that we see in the outside world is a reflection of what's going on in the inside world, whether we like it or not. So Ellev8 is about helping us individually and collectively to be shining our light so that we are really showing up in the darkness and helping to bring light to that.

What do I mean by darkness? When I talk about darkness, I'm referring to whenever we're not feeling "on top of the world", off par. When we feel light in ourselves, everything is flowing, things feel effortless, there's a grace to life. People comment on how well you look or how happy you seem.

The opposite - the darkness - creates a physical sinking in ourselves. It feels as though we're wading through mud, things feel hard and challenging. We dwell on what's not working rather than what is. We might experience physical disease, relationship struggles, work challenges, or financial worries.

But here's the paradox: the only way for us to see light is when there is darkness. So there's a massive leap of faith in finding that shift to lift us through the darkness - or through the muddy waters in the case of a lotus flower - to bring us out into the light.

Together, we'll explore eight essential aspects of your being:

1. 🌱 Your foundation - where fear transforms into trust and safety
2. 💧 Your creative energy - where hidden desires bloom into authentic expression
3. ○ Your personal power - where doubt gives way to quiet confidence
4. 💚 Your heart centre - where old wounds open into deeper connection
5. 🎤 Your voice - where silence transforms into clear truth
6. ◉ Your inner wisdom - where confusion clarifies into knowing
7. ○ Your spiritual connection - where control softens into purpose
8. ∞ Integrating it all.

This journey weaves together ancient wisdom about our energy centres (chakras) with practical, everyday ways to bring that wisdom to life. We'll explore how to balance action with intuition, structure with flow - what I call the Ellev8 philosophy.

But this isn't just another self-help book. Think of it more as a conversation - one where we explore, question, discover, and grow together. By the final page, you won't just understand these concepts - you'll feel them in your very being. You'll notice yourself moving through the world differently, standing in your truth more fully, embracing all of who you are.

Please join me

**With love, light and grace**
**Karen ♥ xxx**

# ACKNOWLEDGMENTS

No journey is ever walked alone, and this book has been shaped by so many hearts and hands.

To my Ellev8 community - you've shown me how powerful it is when we create space for each other to grow and transform. Your willingness to be real, to be vulnerable, to show up exactly as you are - this has taught me more than you know.

To my family - those living and passed - you've given me roots to grow from and wings to fly with. Your support has made everything possible.

To every client who has trusted me with their story - your courage to look deeply at yourselves, to question, to change, to grow... you've helped shape not just this book, but my understanding of what transformation really means.

To my dear friends who've walked this path with me - thank you for the late-night conversations, the honest feedback, the moments of laughter and tears that have enriched this work.

To all my teachers, mentors and coaches over the years and decades - thank you for your insights and for helping me to continuously upgrade (still!).

To Pete Lonton my book writing coach - thank you for always asking the right questions at the right time to lead into deeply meaningful downloads.

And to you, reading these words right now - thank you for being willing to explore your own light, to being open to Ellev8'ing. This book is now yours. Take what resonates, question what challenges you, make it your own. Your journey is unique, and that's exactly as it should be.

# EXECUTIVE SUMMARY

This book is your invitation to transformation - not by becoming someone different, but by illuminating, shining the light on who you truly are.

Through these pages, we'll explore the ancient wisdom of the chakras (your body's energy centres) in practical, everyday ways. We'll discover how to balance action with intuition through the Ellev8 philosophy, where structure and flow come together to create lasting change.

Each chapter guides you through a different aspect of your journey:

1. **Finding Your Foundation** Start with what grounds you. Learn simple practices to transform fear into trust, building the security you need to grow.
2. **Awakening Your Creativity** Explore your natural flow and creative energy, moving past shame into genuine self-expression.
3. **Claiming Your Power** Stand confidently in your truth, transforming self-doubt into quiet, authentic strength.
4. **Opening Your Heart** Heal old wounds and deepen your connections - with yourself and others.
5. **Speaking Your Truth** Find your voice and use it, breaking free from old patterns of silence.

6. ◉ **Trusting Your Wisdom** Learn to recognize and trust your inner knowing - it's been there all along.
7. ◯ **Embracing Something Greater** Connect with your deeper purpose, finding peace in the balance of control and surrender.
8. **Living It** Allowing it all to be as it unfolds

This isn't just information to read - it's an experience to live. Through simple practices, thoughtful reflections, and real-world applications, you'll discover how these ancient teachings can transform your everyday life.

By the time you finish this book, you'll notice subtle but profound shifts in how you move through the world. You'll stand taller, breathe deeper, and trust yourself more fully.

Most importantly, you'll have practical tools and gentle wisdom to support you as you continue growing into your most authentic self.

Ready to begin?

Jot down here how you are feeling about beginning.

A Gift for you to Enhance your Journey

The companion Workbook to Ellev8 Book One "Letting the Light in" is for sale on Amazon and elsewhere but... I would like to give you a copy of the pdf as a Gift to enhance your whole experience as you go on this journey with me.

You can download it via the QR code or at this link:

https://tinyurl.com/Letting-the-Light-in-Workbook

## Chapter 1
# STARTING WITH THE BASICS

*Root Chakra, Grounding in Trust & Security*

---

*"Like the roots of a tree, your foundation determines how high you can grow. Like a well-prepared meal, the right ingredients create nourishment and strength."*

---

## Dear Ellev8'ing One,

Do you ever catch yourself in those quiet moments - perhaps gazing out of your window as morning light fills the sky, or taking in the night air before bed - and sense something stirring within you? A knowing that you're ready for more, ready to step into who you truly are?

Every morning, I open my curtains and take in the view. For me, it's hills and sheep and birdsong, but your view might be city streets coming to life, suburban gardens, open fields or a small patch of sky between buildings. Every evening, I open my window wide, regardless of the weather, and take a moment to be present with whatever the sky offers. These simple practices have taught me something important: transformation isn't about becoming someone new - it's about letting the light illuminate who you've actually been all along.

This book is an invitation to that illumination. Not just to read about it, but to experience it.

Together, we'll work with the ancient wisdom of the chakras - but don't worry, we'll keep this practical and real. Just as I've seen countless times in my work with clients the deepest transformations often happen in the most unlikely moments.

We'll explore eight essential aspects of your being, each one building on the last:

- Your foundation - where we'll transform fear into trust through simple, grounding practices
- Your creative energy - where we'll move past shame into genuine self-expression

- Your personal power - where doubt gives way to quiet confidence
- Your heart - where old hurts can finally heal into deeper connection
- Your voice - where you'll discover the strength to speak your truth
- Your intuition - where you'll learn to trust that inner knowing you've always had
- Your spiritual connection - where control can soften into purpose

Integrating it all
Let's get started

**With love, light and grace**
**Karen xxx**

### Let's Have a Cup of Tea...

In this **busy outward world**, we've grown accustomed to **constant movement**—always striving, always looking ahead. But there is a **gentle yet powerful opportunity** waiting for us:

- *A simple cup of tea.*

It's an **invitation to pause**. To sit down. To **create space** for reflection and conversation.

My radio show, *Around the Table with Karen*, was born from this idea. It provided a space to **shine a light on amazing people doing amazing things**. But more than that, it was a reminder of the **power of simply listening**.

Just by **being present** and **creating space**, we allow **understanding to unfold**.

And this is what grounding is all about.

## The Kitchen as Sanctuary: Finding Security in the Simple Things

You know that moment when you walk into a kitchen where something wonderful is cooking?

That first breath that tells you you're home, you're safe, you're exactly where you need to be?

For me, this happens when I'm cooking with fresh herbs. There's something about the way basil or rosemary release their fragrance that brings me right into the present moment. No rushing ahead, no dwelling on the past - just here, now, with these simple gifts. Breathing it in.

This is what grounding is really about. Not some complicated spiritual practice, but these everyday moments of complete presence. When I'm stirring a pot of soup, chopping vegetables, or making scrambled eggs, my mind naturally settles. My breathing slows. I find myself in a kind of "kitchen meditation" - and trust me, it's often more powerful than trying to sit still on a cushion!

For me, cooking really encapsulates all of this. Even with something as simple as scrambled eggs, the difference between "good" scrambled eggs and "bad" or average scrambled eggs is mindfulness, love and attention. What makes the difference is allowing it to be special, wanting it to be special. And it is being very present with what we're doing, not just slapping it in, beating the eggs up, putting them in the pan, turning away, getting on with something else, coming back. Scrambled eggs can make a great analogy for living! It's a bit like somebody just living a life, getting through it, and then there's really living life.

Being present is such a key for living an Ellev8'ed life, such a key for fulfillment. I've had people laugh when I'm preparing veggies, cutting things up to go into a dish I'm making. Maybe I'm chopping up a stick of celery, and I might use seven eighths of the stick of celery and know, somehow, that's enough, and not to put the rest in. So it's allowing yourself to be really connected with whatever it is you're doing, whether it's cooking, walking, playing with children, being in conversation with someone, really being present, so that you can really connect with the activity or the person.

Think about it - cooking isn't just about following recipes. It's about trust. Trust that the soufflé will rise. Trust that the flavours will develop if we give them time. Trust that even if we make a mistake, we can usually rescue it (and yes, I've had plenty of those moments!).

This is exactly what we're exploring when we talk about feeling secure in life. Just as a good meal needs proper ingredients and patience, building trust in ourselves and life requires:

- Time to let things develop
- Willingness to stay present
- Gentle attention rather than force
- Trust in the process, even when we can't see the end result

You don't need fancy equipment or special skills to start. Just like finding your own morning window ritual, you can create simple kitchen practices that ground you. Maybe it's the way you prepare your morning tea or coffee. Perhaps it's taking three deep breaths before you start cooking. Whatever feels natural to you.

What matters is the presence you bring to these moments. When you're preparing food, really notice what you're doing. Feel the textures, notice the colours, hear the sounds. Let these simple actions bring you home to yourself.

## The Root Chakra: Finding Your Foundation

Let me share something I've noticed over years of working with clients. When someone feels unsettled or anxious, they often reach for a cup of tea first, before saying a word. That simple act of holding a warm cup, feeling its weight, breathing in the steam - it's instinctive. We naturally seek ways to ground ourselves.

This is what the Root Chakra is all about. Now, don't worry if the term 'chakra' feels a bit "out there" - think of it as your foundation, your base, your sense of safety in the world. Just as a tree needs strong roots to grow tall, we need this solid base to truly flourish.

The ancient teachers called it 'Muladhara' - but let's talk about what this really means in our everyday lives. It's about:

- Feeling safe in your own skin
- Knowing you have what you need
- Trusting that you can handle what comes
- Being present in your body and this moment

When this foundation is strong, you'll notice:

- You sleep better
- Your breathing is deeper
- Money decisions feel clearer
- Your body feels more like home
- Change feels manageable rather than threatening

But here's what I often see in my work: When we're running on empty, constantly rushing, or worried about basic needs, this foundation gets shaky. You might notice:

- Your mind races at night
- You're always slightly on edge
- Small problems feel overwhelming
- You struggle to stay present
- Making decisions becomes harder

Remember that simple practice of taking a moment at your window? It's not just a nice ritual - it's a way of reminding your body and mind that you're safe, supported, here.

The fascinating thing about working with your Root Chakra is that simple practices often work better than complicated ones. Just like the satisfaction of preparing a simple meal, grounding yourself doesn't need to be complex.

## Practical Ways to Strengthen Your Foundation

You know how different it feels to drink tea mindfully - really noticing the warmth of the cup, the aroma, the taste - compared to gulping it down while checking your phone? That same principle of presence is at the heart of building a stronger foundation.

Let me share some simple practices that really work. These aren't complicated techniques - they're more like coming home to yourself:

**Your Morning Moment** Find your own way to greet the day. Maybe it's standing barefoot on your floor for a moment, feeling its support beneath you. Taking three breaths where you actually feel your breath. Noticing what's around you - the light, the sounds, the temperature. This isn't about positive thinking - it's about being present in your body, in this moment.

**Kitchen Presence** Next time you're preparing food - even if it's just making toast - try this: Feel your feet on the floor. Notice the textures, sounds and smells of what you're doing. Let the simple actions of cooking anchor you in the now. If your mind wanders (and it will!), just come back to the sensations.

**The Body Check-In** This one's perfect with that first cup of tea or coffee. As you sit, feel where your body makes contact with the chair. Notice any places of tension. No need to change anything - just notice. Like watching the sky change, just observe what's there.

But what about when things get tough?

When anxiety rises or you're feeling untethered, here's what works:

**Get Back to Basics**

- Are you hungry? Eat something nourishing (not something sugary)
- Thirsty? Drink some water (not caffeine)
- Tired? Rest if you can even if it's just a few minutes or do a short relaxation exercise
- Feeling "foggy"? Open a window or step outside

**Use Your Physical Senses**

Tune into:

- What you can see
- What you can feel
- What you can hear
- What you can smell
- What you can taste

This isn't just a clever exercise - it literally brings you back into your body, into this moment.

# Letting the Light In

Before we move to our tea ritual, I want to share a poem with you. It speaks to this journey we're beginning together - how even the smallest opening can lead to profound change.

**"Letting the Light In"**
*A poem by Karen Kennaby*

First, a tiny speck
Inconceivable that it could light up so much darkness
But, while the light stays constant
Its impact grows as our eyes adjust
Now we see more, in the darkness
Now we see other lights
Other flames
Shining, glowing
More and more
Until we realise that
One little light, one tiny speck
Has overcome the darkness
Cracks are where the light comes in, sings Leonard Cohen
Yes, the light comes in every chance it gets
It wants to overcome the darkness
And we, you and I, get to be the light
If we choose
To let the light in

## Coming Home to Your Self

You know in the evenings when I open my window? Sometimes there are stars scattered across the sky, sometimes darkness or clouds. But I know the stars are always there, whether I can see them or not.

This is what I've learned about feeling secure and grounded - it's not about everything being perfect or having all the answers. It's about knowing that beneath any temporary storms, your foundation remains.

Building this foundation isn't a one-time achievement. It's more like my morning and evening practices - something we return to, day after day. Sometimes it feels natural and easy. Other times we have to remind ourselves to pause, to breathe, to come back to centre.

Remember:

- Security isn't about having everything figured out
- Stability can exist even in times of change
- Your body knows how to ground itself - our job is to listen
- Small, consistent practices matter more than grand gestures

Before we move on to the next chapter, I invite you to choose one small way to strengthen your foundation today. Maybe it's taking three conscious breaths before your morning coffee. Perhaps it's feeling your feet on the floor while waiting for the kettle to boil. Or simply pausing to notice where you are, right now.

What matters isn't how big or small the practice is - it's the presence and intention you bring to it.

Are you ready to explore what comes next?

## Taking a Deeper Look

Let's pause for a moment, like we would with a cup of tea. In my experience, the right questions can open doors we didn't even know were there. Not to find perfect answers, but to understand ourselves better.

Think about...

1. Where in your life do you feel unstable or uncertain? Notice if there are particular areas where you sense that shakiness in your foundation.

2. How does your relationship with food and nourishment reflect your sense of security? The way we eat - hurried or mindful, nourishing or neglectful - often mirrors our relationship with security.

3. What fears might be keeping you from feeling grounded? Naming them is the first step to working with them.

4. What rituals or practices make you feel safe and supported? These might be as simple as your morning cup of tea or as structured as a meditation practice.

5. How do you typically handle stress, uncertainty, or setbacks? Do you have patterns that serve you well, and others that might need gentle adjustment?

6. What simple activities bring you peace? Perhaps cooking, walking, gardening, or something else entirely? These everyday practices can be powerful grounding tools.

7. How might you build a stronger sense of trust in yourself and the world? Trust is often built through small, consistent experiences of safety and reliability.

8. What is one small action you can take today to feel more grounded? Sometimes the smallest steps make the biggest difference.

These aren't questions to answer all at once. Let them sit with you. Notice what comes up as you go about your day. You might be surprised by what you discover.

And remember - this exploration isn't about finding what's wrong. It's about understanding where you are, so you can build an even stronger foundation.

Use this space to jot down anything that comes up for you.

# Recipe:
# The Perfect Cup of Tea -
# A Grounding Ritual

A cup of tea is more than just a drink—it's a moment of stillness, a pause in the rush of life. Making tea teaches us patience, presence, and the art of waiting for the right moment.

Let's make this simple act into a grounding practice:

**Boil with intention.** Don't rush. As the kettle heats, take three deep breaths. Feel your feet on the floor. Notice the sounds, the steam beginning to rise.

**Choose mindfully.** Select your tea with care. Notice its scent. Feel the warmth of the cup in your hands. This moment is just for you.

**Steep with patience.** Like trust, tea takes time. Watch the colour develop. No need to rush. Let the warmth of the cup spread through your hands.

**Sip with presence.** Feel the warmth. Notice the flavours. Let each sip be a moment of coming home to your self (I like to split yourself into two words for emphasis)

## Chapter 2
# PHASES OF LIFE
*The Sacral Chakra, Creativity & Flow*

---

*"Life is what happens when we're busy making plans. Life leaves clues—we just have to be willing to follow them."*

---

### Dear Ellev8'ing One,

Have you ever noticed how life has its own timing? Sometimes when we're pushing hardest for something to happen, life has other plans. And often, looking back, we can see why - though it rarely makes sense at the time.

Let's talk about something that's at the heart of all my work - the Ellev8 symbol. You know it as the infinity sign: ∞. But it's more than just a symbol - it's a way of understanding how life actually works.

The universe loves speed. When we allow ourselves to take too long to go over and over and over something, we procrastinate, we get into our heads, whereas when we act on that inner knowing, that impulse, that intuition, that nudge, and we take action on it, that is the action to take. Yes, we might have to reflect and consider what the exact steps are, but really following through quickly brings about the change that we're looking for.

Liz Gilbert in her book, Big Magic, talks about the fact that ideas come to you, but if you don't take them up - creative ideas this is - if you don't take them up, then they'll go to someone else. And it does feel a bit like that. I think we've probably all had incidences where we've had what we thought was a brilliant idea, but then we didn't act on it. And then a short time later, somebody else does exactly that. They create exactly what we'd thought of, and we think 'how did they copy me?' They didn't copy us. It's in the ether. And if we don't do it, someone else will.

Explore with me!

### With love, light and grace
### Karen 🖤 xxx

## Phases of Life

Look at it for a moment. See how it flows in a continuous loop, never stopping, always moving? That's exactly how life energy moves through us. Sometimes we're in our action mode - getting things done, making decisions, pushing forward. Other times we're in our receptive mode - listening, feeling, allowing things to unfold.

This isn't about gender - every one of us has both these energies:

- That focused drive that gets things done (traditionally called masculine or yang energy)
- That intuitive wisdom that knows when to wait (traditionally called feminine or yin energy)

The trick isn't choosing one over the other - it's learning to dance between them. Sometimes we need to act, other times we need to listen. Sometimes we need to lead, other times we need to flow.

Think about the most effective people you know. They probably know how to be both strong and gentle, both decisive and receptive. They understand that true power comes from knowing when to use each energy.

Take someone like Michelle Obama. Yes, she's incredibly focused and driven - that's her masculine energy at work. But watch her in action and you'll see how she leads with heart, how she knows when to stand firm and when to show vulnerability. Or consider Serena Williams on the tennis court - pure power and discipline, yes, but also an incredible sense of timing and flow. These women haven't succeeded by pushing all the time or by only going with the flow - they've mastered the dance between both energies.

## Life's Natural Rhythms

Just as we noticed in Chapter 1 how grounding happens naturally - through simple acts like making tea or feeling our feet on the floor - this dance of energies is happening all around us. You see it in the changing seasons, in the cycles of the moon, in the ebb and flow of the tides.

Traditional wisdom and modern psychology, tell us that our lives move in seven-year cycles. Each phase brings its own gifts and challenges:

1. **0-7 years** – The foundation: security, belonging, and emotional trust.
2. **7-14 years** – Identity formation: learning who we are in relation to the world.
3. **14-21 years** – Independence: exploring creativity, relationships, and self-expression.
4. **21-28 years** – Establishment: career, relationships, creating our adult lives.
5. **28-35 years** – Reevaluation: questioning purpose, passions, and direction.
6. **35-42 years** – Refinement: deeper creativity, wisdom, and authenticity.
7. **42-49 years** – Expansion: letting go of old narratives, stepping into true self.
8. **49+ years** – Mastery: embracing wisdom, leading, and living fully.

Every 7 years, we experience **a shift—a chance to evolve into a new version of ourselves**. When we resist change, we feel stuck. When we embrace it, **we open ourselves to deeper creativity and purpose**.

This cyclical nature of life is reflected in the **Ellev8 Infinity Symbol—an endless loop of transformation, creation, and elevation**.

## The Sacral Chakra: Your Creative Centre

Remember how we explored the Root Chakra as your foundation? Well, if that's your base, think of the Sacral Chakra as your creative centre. It sits just below your navel, and it's all about flow - in your emotions, your creativity, your relationships, your whole way of being in the world.

The ancient teachers called it 'Svadhisthana' - but let's talk about what this really means in your everyday life. This is where:

- Your creative impulses come from (and not just artistic creativity)
- Your emotions flow (or sometimes get stuck)
- Your sense of pleasure and joy lives
- Your ability to go with life's flow (or resist it) begins

When this energy centre is flowing freely, you might notice:

- Ideas come more easily
- You feel more emotionally balanced
- You can adapt to change without getting thrown off
- Life feels more joyful, more pleasurable

- You trust your intuition while still staying practical

But when it's blocked (and we all get blocked sometimes), you might find:

- Your creativity feels stuck
- Your emotions feel either overwhelming or shut down
- You resist change, even when you know it's needed
- Joy and pleasure feel hard to access
- You're either all logic or all feeling, with no balance

## Practical Ways to Get Your Creative Energy Flowing

You know those mornings when you wake up and everything just flows? Ideas come easily, decisions feel natural, you're in sync with life? That's your creative energy in full flow. The good news is, we don't have to wait for those moments to happen by chance - we can create them.

Let me share some practices that really work. Just like our grounding techniques, these aren't complicated - they're about working with what's natural:

**Morning Pages** This is one of my favorite practices, it comes from the seminal book on creativity "The Artist's Way" by Julia Cameron. Before you check your phone, before you start your day, just write. Three pages of whatever comes to mind - no judging, no editing, no trying to make it good. It might be complaints, dreams, shopping lists - doesn't matter. What matters is letting it flow.

Creativity is a huge way to connect with your inside self, to go deeply connected, because it gets you out of your head. It's that virtuous circle, actually, because when you're doing something creative, you're out of your head. And when you're out of your head, you can do something creative.

**The Water Practice** Water teaches us about flow better than anything else. Whether you're in the shower, washing dishes, or just drinking a glass of water - notice how water always finds its path. It never fights gravity; it simply flows around obstacles. Let water remind you of your own natural ability to flow. This is something I always take delight in on my walks - seeing the way the streams constantly change course to continue to flow.

**Movement and Play** We often try to think our way through creative blocks, but the answer is usually in moving our bodies. Put on music and dance while you're making breakfast. Stretch while waiting for the kettle to boil. Go for a walk. Skip down the street (yes, really!). Movement shifts energy faster than thinking ever can.

But what about when you're really stuck?

When creativity feels blocked, emotions are overwhelming, or life feels like it's fighting you, try this:

**First, Check Your Basic Needs**
- Are you trying to be creative on an empty stomach?
- Have you moved your body today?
- When did you last drink water?
- Could you use some fresh air?

**Then, try this Simple Flow Practice**

Sit quietly and notice:
- The sounds around you

- The things you can feel
- The colours you can see
- The different temperatures on your skin
- The rhythm (maybe your heartbeat or breath)

This isn't just a mindfulness exercise - it's about getting you out of your head and back into the flow of life.

## Taking a Deeper Look

Just as we sat with questions about grounding in Chapter 1, let's pause here and explore your relationship with creativity and flow. Not to find perfect answers, but to understand yourself better.

Think about...

1. Where in your life might you be resisting flow? Sometimes we hold on tightly to control even when letting go would serve us better.

2. How do you typically handle change and transitions? Do you embrace them, resist them, or something in between?

3. What creative passions have you ignored or suppressed? Perhaps things you loved as a child but set aside, or new interests you've been curious about but haven't explored.

4. How do you balance masculine (action) and feminine (intuition) energy in your life? Where might you need more focused drive, and where might you benefit from more receptivity?

5. What season or 7-year cycle do you feel you're currently in? What might it be teaching you about yourself and your journey?

6. How could you embrace play and spontaneity more in your everyday life? Where have you perhaps become too serious or structured?

7. What emotions are you avoiding? How might you express them creatively rather than keeping them bottled up?

8. What is one thing you could create for the pure joy of it - with no goal, no expectation of it being "good," simply for the pleasure of creating?

These aren't questions to answer all at once. Let them sit with you, like tea steeping. Notice what comes up as you go about your day. You might be surprised by what you discover.

Use this space to jot down anything that comes up for you.

# Closing Thoughts: Dancing with Life's Flow

You know those evenings when I open my window? Sometimes the night is alive with sound and movement - wind in the trees, distant traffic, the last birds settling. Other times it's completely still. Each moment different, each moment perfect in its own way.

This is what I've learned about creativity and flow - it's not about forcing ourselves to always be 'on', always creating, always moving forward. It's about recognizing the natural rhythm of things. Sometimes we're in full creative flow, other times we're gathering new experiences, and sometimes we're simply resting.

Remember:

- You don't have to be creating all the time to be creative
- Change isn't just inevitable - it's how we grow
- Your body knows about flow - just watch how you breathe without thinking
- Small moments of play matter more than grand creative gestures

Before we move on to the next chapter, I invite you to notice one way you naturally flow in your life. Maybe it's in the way you move to music when no one's watching. Perhaps it's in how you arrange things in your home. Or in the way you naturally find solutions when you stop trying so hard.

What matters isn't how big or dramatic your creative expression is - it's about trusting your own natural rhythm.

Are you ready to explore what comes next?

# Recipe:
# A Lesson in Flow
# Mindful Risotto

You can't rush a risotto, and you can only make a good one with love. That's what makes it such a beautiful practice in presence and flow. Each step asks for your attention, your patience, your willingness to respond to what's happening in the moment.

**Serves:** 2 (generously)

## Ingredients

- 2 tablespoons olive oil
- 2 tablespoons butter
- 1 clove garlic, chopped
- 1 medium onion, finely chopped
- 200g (7oz) risotto rice
- 1 small glass white wine (about 125ml or 4 fl oz)
- About 750ml (1¼ pints) simmering vegetable stock
- Salt & pepper to taste

## For finishing

- Your choice of wild mushrooms, shrimp, or spring vegetables (pre-cooked)
- Grated parmesan
- Chopped chives (optional)

## The Practice

Begin by creating your space. Have everything ready, stock simmering, ingredients prepared. Like any creative endeavor, good preparation allows you to fully enter the flow.

1. Melt the butter with olive oil, then add your onion and garlic. Notice how their aroma fills the kitchen as they soften to translucency.
2. Add the rice, stirring for about 3 minutes. Feel how it changes texture, becoming slightly translucent at the edges.
3. Now comes the dance - add wine first, let it bubble and absorb. Then begin adding stock, one ladle at a time. Each addition is like a breath - pour, stir, wait, notice. Don't rush. Let each ladle of stock be absorbed before adding the next.
4. Keep this rhythm until the rice tells you it's done - when it's tender but still has a slight bite, and can't absorb any more liquid.
5. Fold in your chosen ingredients, letting them warm through. Finish with parmesan and chives if using.

This isn't just cooking - it's a lesson in being present, in working with rather than against the natural flow of things. You can't force risotto to cook faster, just as you can't force creativity or personal growth. But give it time, attention, and love, and it will transform into something beautiful.

# Chapter 3
# WE'RE ALL BROKEN, AND WE'RE ALSO ALL WHOLE

*The Solar Plexus Chakra, Confidence & Personal Power*

---

*"You are powerful beyond measure. The question is, do you believe it?"*

---

### *Dear Ellev8'ing One,*

Have you ever noticed how the most powerful people you meet aren't the ones who pretend to be perfect? They're the ones who've been through something, learned from it, and aren't afraid to let that wisdom shine through.

Rumi captures this perfectly: "The wound is the place where the light enters you." Leonard Cohen echoes this truth when he sings, "There's a crack, a crack in everything, that's where the light gets in."

This chapter is about discovering your own power - not by hiding your struggles or pretending to be unbreakable, but by embracing your whole story, cracks and all.

### *With love, light and grace*
### *Karen ♥ xxx*

# Authentic Power

Just as we explored how to ground ourselves in Chapter 1, and how to flow with life's rhythms in Chapter 2, now we're learning to stand in our power. But this isn't about powering over others or pushing your way through life. It's about something much more authentic - the quiet confidence that comes from knowing and accepting all of who you are.

The Solar Plexus Chakra, which we'll explore together, is where this inner fire lives. It's the energy centre that governs:

- Your sense of self-worth (not the kind that needs proving, but the kind that simply knows)
- Your ability to take action (not from fear, but from clarity)
- Your presence in the world (not a mask you wear, but your genuine self shining through)

Think about those moments when you feel most authentically yourself. Maybe it's when you're doing something you love, or speaking about something you deeply believe in, or simply being with people who know and accept you completely. That feeling of being fully present, fully yourself - that's your Solar Plexus energy in flow.

But here's what often trips us up: somewhere along the way, most of us learned that power means never showing weakness. Never admitting doubt. Never letting people see our struggles.

The Japanese art of Kintsugi tells us something different. When precious pottery breaks, instead of hiding the cracks or throwing it away, artists repair it with gold. The breaks become the most beautiful part of the piece - telling the story of its resilience, its history, its journey.

What if we looked at ourselves the same way? What if every challenge we've faced, every setback, every moment that cracked us open - what if these weren't flaws to hide but wisdom to share?

I see this in my work all the time. People come thinking they need to fix something broken in themselves. But often, what they really need is to understand that those very breaks - those experiences that cracked them open - have created space for more light to enter.

I know the power of embracing our whole story personally. A couple of years ago, I was talking about writing a book about the roller coaster of my life. I thought I was fine about some of the most poignant aspects of my life (which I'll share another time), but my book coach Pete asked others in our group, 'Is anybody else buying this, that Karen's fine?' They weren't. That conversation helped me go very, very deep - right down to the bottom of the ocean, to see what was underneath everything. Only then could I come back up. But I had to really 'go there' first.

Think about it:

- That time you "failed" taught you resilience
- That heartbreak showed you what you truly value
- That setback made you reassess what really matters
- That loss opened you to deeper compassion

This isn't about celebrating suffering - it's about recognizing that our challenges shape us in ways that make us more whole, more real, more authentically powerful.

As Marianne Williamson reminds us: "Our deepest fear is not that we are inadequate. Our deepest fear is that we are powerful beyond measure. It is our light, not our darkness that most frightens us. We ask ourselves, 'Who am I to be brilliant, gorgeous, talented, fabulous?' Actually, who are you not to be? You are a child of God. Your playing small does not serve the world. There is nothing enlightened about shrinking so that other people won't feel insecure around you. We are all meant to shine, as children do... And as we let our own light shine, we unconsciously give other people permission to do the same."

Think about that for a moment. What if your power isn't just for you? What if by stepping fully into who you are, you're actually creating space for others to do the same?

## Reclaiming Our Light: Women Who Stepped into Their Strength

It's one thing to talk about power in the abstract, but what does it look like in real women's lives? Throughout history, women have been told to stay quiet, play small, and not take up space. And yet, time and again, we've witnessed the power of women reclaiming their voices, their power, and their identities.

Think about **Maya Angelou** — truly a woman who rose. She endured trauma, racism, and oppression—and yet, she became one of the most powerful literary voices in history. After being silenced by childhood abuse, she refused to remain voiceless. She wrote, she spoke, she reclaimed herself.

As she wisely said, "There is no greater agony than bearing an untold story inside you."

Or consider **Malala Yousafzai** – the girl who refused to be silenced. At just 15 years old, she was shot by the Taliban for fighting for girls' education. Many would have retreated into silence—but she used that moment to step into her greatest power. Now, she is a global force for education and empowerment.

**Frida Kahlo** showed us another path – turning pain into power. Her life was full of physical suffering, heartbreak, and challenges. But instead of hiding her pain, she painted it—transforming her trauma into art, using her wounds as a bridge to connect with others.

And then there's **Oprah Winfrey** – from trauma to triumph. Abused as a child and told she wasn't good enough, she could have lived in the shadow of her past. Instead, she claimed her voice and her presence, becoming one of the most influential women in history.

As she reminds us, "Think like a queen. A queen is not afraid to fail. Failure is another stepping stone to greatness."

These women prove that power isn't about perfection. It's about reclamation, resilience, and the courage to be seen. They didn't succeed despite their wounds – in many ways, they transformed because of them, letting the light shine through their cracks, just as we talked about with Kintsugi.

## Working with Your Power

Here's something I've noticed in my own life and my work - often when we start to shine more brightly, when we begin to take up our full space in the world, two things happen:

First, we might feel scared. That's normal. Just like our eyes need time to adjust to bright light, we need time to adjust to our own power.

Second, something magical occurs - other people start to shift too. It's as if our permission to be fully ourselves gives them permission to do the same.

This is what makes working with the Solar Plexus energy so important and exciting. It's not just about personal confidence - it's about creating ripples of possibility around us.

Let's look at some practical ways to work with this:

**1. Start Your Day with Power**

Remember our morning practices? Add this: As you start your day, take one deep breath and say to yourself "I give myself permission to shine today." Simple, but notice how it feels.

**2. Turn "Who am I to..." into "Why Not Me?"**

Next time you hear that voice asking "Who am I to speak up/take the lead/share my ideas?" try answering it: "Why not me? What if my voice is exactly what's needed?"

**3. Create a Power Pause**

When you feel yourself shrinking or holding back, pause. Put your hand on your solar plexus. Take three breaths. Remember: you're not just doing this for yourself - your courage creates courage in others.

Trust comes from an inner knowing. We gain trust when we are deeply connected to ourselves, to who we are. When we are connected to source, whatever we call that, and it might be God, it might be the universe, it might be life with a capital L, it might be Great Spirit, whatever it is that we know is much bigger than us.

And when we get into that place of trust, what happens is, we are actually kept a lot more safe. We are likely to tune into different energies that will bring up warning signs, for example about a person or a place. So really, and truly, it's a very clear guidance system, if we really do have the deep connection.

Whether that's meditation for you, whether it's journaling, whether it's walking in nature, whatever it is, whether it's cold water swimming, it's whatever it is for you, it's that place where you go to your mind is completely out of the way, you're completely connected. And then the trust is there, because you know, that what is coming up is pure and clean and clear.

## The Power of Both/And

Just as we learn to balance our breath - both inhaling and exhaling, both energising and calming - we can learn to balance our interactions with others:

- Being both grounded in our truth AND open to others' perspectives
- Staying both true to ourselves AND connected to those we love
- Holding both our boundaries AND our compassion

This balance becomes even more important in today's world, where big issues like Covid-19, Brexit or political choices can divide families and friendships in moments. We often see people moving quickly to opposing corners, losing sight of the human beings behind the viewpoints.

This is where our grounding practices become vital:

**Physically Anchoring**
- Keep breathing deeply
- Feel your feet on the ground
- Notice when your body tenses in reaction
- Stay present rather than rushing to respond

**Using Emotional Intelligence**
- Remember the humanity in everyone
- Notice when you're moving into judgment
- Choose understanding over winning
- Trust that it's possible to disagree with someone's view while still honouring their worth as a person

## Navigating Challenging Conversations

When big issues arise - whether at the family dinner table or in work meetings - here's how to stay both grounded and open:

**Before the Conversation**
- Take those deep breaths
- Feel your feet firmly on the ground
- Remind yourself: the goal is understanding, not converting
- Set an intention to see the human being, the person, behind the viewpoint

**During Difficult Moments**
- Keep breathing deeply
- Stay aware of the chair or ground supporting you
- Notice if your body is tensing
- Remember you can pause before responding

- Use phrases like:
    - "Help me understand your perspective"
    - "I see this differently, but I'm interested in your view"
    - "We might not agree, but I value our relationship"
    - "Let's focus on what we share"

**When You Feel Triggered**

- Return to your breath
- Feel your feet on the floor
- Notice where you're holding tension
- Remember: you can be right or you can be love
- Ask yourself: "What matters more here - winning this point or maintaining connection?"

This doesn't mean:

- Abandoning your values
- Accepting harmful views
- Staying silent about important issues
- Letting others cross your boundaries

It means:

- Staying grounded in your truth while remaining curious
- Choosing your moments wisely
- Speaking with clarity and compassion
- Remembering that most people are doing their best with what they know

## Moving Forward with Grace

After a heated conversation, disagreement or stand-off, we have choices about how to move forward. This is where real power shows itself - not in winning arguments, but in maintaining connection while staying true to ourselves.

### The Next Day
- Return to your morning practices
- Notice any residual tension in your body
- Keep breathing deeply
- Remember: yesterday's heat doesn't have to determine today's temperature (I love this phrase!)

### Rebuilding Bridges
- Make eye contact
- Share a smile
- Engage in simple, everyday interactions
- Focus on what you share rather than what divides you
- Let your natural warmth flow again

### Stay Grounded In:
- Your values
- Your truth
- Your right to your perspective
- Your choice to prioritise connection

Remember:
- You can disagree without disconnecting
- You can hold your truth while allowing others theirs
- You can choose peace without compromising your integrity
- You can be both strong and gentle

## Taking a Deeper Look

Just as we did in earlier chapters, let's pause for a moment to reflect more deeply. These questions aren't about finding perfect answers but about exploring your relationship with your own power:

Think about, or journal on...

1. What parts of yourself have you disowned or hidden? Perhaps qualities that didn't seem acceptable or that felt too vulnerable to show.

2. What experiences in your past do you still see as "failures" rather than lessons? How might the story change if you viewed them through the lens of growth?

3. How can you begin to reclaim your confidence and self-worth in areas where you've given your power away?

4. What does the Japanese concept of seven generations teach you about your own past and future? How might you honour both where you've come from and what you're creating for those who follow?

5. What limiting belief has kept you from fully stepping into your power? Often these are statements that begin with a version of "I'm not enough..." or "Who am I to..."

6. How do you truly feel about being seen and heard? Notice if there's excitement, fear, or both when you think about taking up your space.

7. If you filled your past wounds with gold like Kintsugi, how would you tell your story differently? What wisdom might shine through those very places?

8. What is one bold step you can take today - however small - to reclaim your power?

Just as with our previous reflections, let these questions sit with you. Notice what emerges without forcing answers. Sometimes the most powerful insights come when we simply create space for them.

Use this space to jot down anything that comes up for you.

# Closing Thoughts: Embracing Your Whole Self

True power isn't about being perfect or unbreakable. It's about embracing all of who you are - those moments when you feel strong and those moments when you feel vulnerable. Those times when you know exactly what to say and those times when you need to pause and breathe.

Remember:

- Your power includes both your strength and your sensitivity
- Your voice matters, even when it shakes
- Your presence makes a difference, even in silence
- Your way of being in the world is needed, just as it is

Like those golden repairs in Kintsugi pottery, or the marbled effect in our Eton Mess recipe, sometimes what we think of as flaws become the most beautiful part of who we are.

Before we move on to the next chapter, I invite you to notice one way you've been trying to hide your cracks rather than fill them with gold. What if those very cracks are where your light shines through most brightly?

Are you ready to explore what comes next?

# Recipe:
# A Lesson in Perfect Imperfection
# Eton Mess

There's something wonderfully symbolic about Eton Mess. Its origin story tells us a lot about making the best of what life brings us - when a pristine strawberry pavlova was dropped at an Eton v Harrow cricket match in the late 19th century, rather than waste it, they simply scooped it up and served it in bowls. What could have been seen as a disaster became a beloved dessert!

This is exactly what we've been talking about - how our 'broken' parts, our messy moments, can become something beautiful. Just like the golden repairs in Kintsugi pottery, sometimes things come together perfectly in their imperfection.

## Ingredients

- 170g/6oz unrefined golden caster sugar
- 3 large egg whites
- 450g/1lb strawberries
- 1 tablespoon unrefined icing sugar
- 570ml/1 pint double cream

## For the Meringues

1. Whisk the egg whites until they form soft peaks. Add the caster sugar gradually, continuing to whisk until thoroughly mixed.

2. Place rounded spoonfuls of the mixture on a lined baking tray and bake for an hour at 135°C/275°F. Leave the meringues to dry out overnight or at least several hours.

## Creating the Mess

1. Mash half the strawberries and mix with the icing sugar
2. Chop the remaining strawberries
3. Whip the double cream
4. Break the meringues into roughly 2.5cm/1 inch pieces
5. In a mixing bowl, combine the broken meringues and chopped strawberries
6. Fold in the cream
7. Gently fold in all but 2 tablespoons of the mashed strawberries to create a marbled effect
8. Place in your serving dish and spoon the remaining mashed strawberries over the top

Serve immediately.

(And yes, you can use ready-made meringues - sometimes making life easier is definitely the wisest choice!)

The beauty of this dessert is that it can't go wrong - it's meant to be messy! Just like life's most meaningful moments, it's not about perfection but about how things come together in their own unique way.

## Chapter 4
# HEARING WHERE YOU ARE

*The Heart Chakra, Compassion & Connection*

> *"Being human is a messy business. Like a kitchen after a wonderful feast - the beauty isn't in the perfect presentation, but in the evidence of a life fully lived."*

### Dear Ellev8'ing One,

Have you ever caught yourself responding "I'm fine" when someone asks how you are, even when you're anything but fine? That moment when your outside voice says one thing, but your heart whispers another entirely?

I was standing at my kitchen window just yesterday, watching rain streak down the glass. Someone had asked how I was feeling about a challenging situation, and I'd automatically answered "I'm fine" - that universal code for "please don't ask more." But as I stood there, hands wrapped around my tea mug, I had to smile at my own reflection. Who was I kidding? Who was I trying to fool?

The truth is, sometimes I am a storm inside while appearing calm on the surface. Sometimes I struggle to bridge the gap between what I show the world and what I truly feel. And I know I'm not alone in this - we all do it. We present versions of ourselves that seem collected and together, because admitting the truth feels too vulnerable, too exposed.

But what if the heart's greatest strength isn't in appearing perfect or "fine" at all? What if it's in the courage to acknowledge the cracks, the wounds, the beautiful mess of being human?

On that note, let's continue as we explore the implications of the heart chakra

### With love, light and grace
### Karen 🤍 xxx

## Embracing Your Humanity

This is where we find ourselves as we explore the Heart Chakra – or Anahata, as the ancient teachers called it. If the Root Chakra grounds us in safety, the Sacral Chakra connects us to our creativity and flow, and the Solar Plexus Chakra empowers us to stand in our truth – then the Heart Chakra is where we truly learn to embrace our full humanity, both the light and the shadow.

Think of the Heart Chakra as the great bridge in your energy system – connecting your physical, earthly nature with your spiritual, intuitive self. Located at the centre of your chest, it's where:

- 🤍 You embrace your complete humanity – both the beauty and the mess
- 🤍 You find the courage to acknowledge pain instead of running from it
- 🤍 You discover how to reclaim love, even after you've been hurt

When this energy centre flows freely, you might notice:

- A deep connection to others without losing yourself
- Compassion balanced with healthy boundaries
- The ability to give and receive love without fear

But when it's blocked (and yes, we all experience blocks sometimes), you might find:

- A fear of intimacy or vulnerability
- Difficulty letting go of resentment
- A sense of emotional numbness or disconnection

This chapter is about hearing where you truly are, not where you wish you were or where others expect you to be. It's about finding the extraordinary strength that comes from embracing your whole heart – cracks, scars and all.

## The 'FINE' Principle: When "Fine" Is Anything But

You know how sometimes the most important conversations happen in the kitchen? There's something about chopping vegetables or stirring a pot that allows truth to emerge in an informal way that might otherwise stay hidden.

I was making soup with a dear friend once, something simple with whatever we had on hand. As we chopped and stirred, she suddenly looked up and said, "I always say I'm fine, but I don't even know what fine means anymore." That simple admission opened a conversation that had been waiting to happen for months.

This is what I've come to call the FINE Principle – when "fine" actually stands for:

- False – We tell ourselves and others something that isn't true, simply to avoid discomfort
- Interpretation – We see situations through the lens of past fears rather than present reality
- Negative – We focus on what might go wrong instead of what could go right
- Emotions – We suppress what we truly feel because facing it seems too painful

Think about it – how often do you use "fine" as a shield? I know I do it. We all do. But here's what I've learned: every time we say we're "fine" when we're not, we place another brick in the wall around our heart.

A number of years ago, I went through a particularly challenging time. When people asked how I was doing, "I'm fine" became my mantra. I think I believed that if I said it enough, it might actually become true. But inside, I was anything but fine. I was carrying grief, uncertainty, and a deep fear of what might come next.

It wasn't until I sat with my best friend, sharing a cup of tea, that something shifted. Instead of saying "I'm fine," I finally whispered the truth: "I'm struggling." Those two words felt like removing a heavy coat I'd been wearing in summer - suddenly I could breathe again. Tears poured down my cheeks but they released something within me. The moment I acknowledged where I truly was - not where I wished I was - something opened in my heart.

That's what this chapter is really about - having the courage to hear where you actually are, rather than where you think you should be.

## The Heart Chakra: Where Connection Begins

Remember how we explored the foundation of the Root Chakra, the creative flow of the Sacral Chakra, and the personal power of the Solar Plexus Chakra? Well, the Heart Chakra builds on all of these. It sits at the centre of your chest - that place you naturally touch when something moves you deeply.

The ancient teachers called it 'Anahata' - which means "unhurt" or "unbeaten." Isn't that beautiful? No matter what life has thrown at you, this centre of love remains fundamentally whole, fundamentally unbeaten. It might be temporarily closed or protected, but it's never truly broken.

In our everyday lives, the Heart Chakra is where:

- We connect deeply with others while honouring ourselves
- We learn to balance giving and receiving
- We cultivate compassion - for others and ourselves
- We transform pain into wisdom

When this energy centre is flowing freely, you might notice:

- Relationships feel nourishing rather than draining
- Forgiveness comes more naturally (including self-forgiveness)
- You can be vulnerable without feeling unsafe
- Life feels rich with meaningful connections

But when it's blocked (and we all experience blocks sometimes), you might find:

- A fear of getting hurt keeps you from opening up
- Past hurts feel impossible to release
- You either give too much or struggle to receive
- Meaningful connection feels elusive or frightening

Think of your Heart Chakra like the kitchen in your home. When a kitchen is functioning well, it's the heart of the house - where nourishment is created, where people gather, where life happens in all its messy glory. But when something's off in the kitchen - perhaps it's cluttered, or the oven isn't working, or there's no space to move freely - the whole house feels the impact.

Similarly, when your Heart Chakra is flowing freely, your entire being benefits. When it's blocked, everything feels a bit off balance.

## What's Really Going On? Hearing Your Heart's Truth

One of the most powerful practices I've learned over the years is to gently question myself when I automatically respond "I'm fine." To pause, like I would when tasting something I'm cooking, and ask: "Is that really true? What am I really feeling? What's actually happening in my heart right now?"

I invite you to try this with me. Take a moment, perhaps with a cup of tea in hand, and ask yourself:

- "Am I telling the truth about where I am right now?" Not where you should be, or where others expect you to be - but where you actually are.
- "What fears might be shaping my choices?" Sometimes we're so used to certain fears that we don't even recognise them as fears anymore - they just feel like "the way things are."
- "What would happen if I stopped pretending to be fine?" Not that you need to announce your struggles to everyone - but what might shift if you at least acknowledged them to yourself?

I've found that true healing, true connection, and true love begin when we have the courage to acknowledge where we are - even when (perhaps especially when) it's messy.

# Reclaiming Your Story: Finding Gold in the Difficult Emotions

You know how some of the most delicious recipes come from using everything - even the parts we might normally throw away? That tough herb stem might add the deepest flavour to the stock. The bread that's gone slightly stale makes the most exquisite toast when drizzled with olive oil.

I've come to see our difficult emotions in a similar way. Those feelings we're often taught to discard or ignore - shame, guilt, heartbreak, regret - actually contain some of our most potent wisdom.

Think about it:

Shame often points to where we need self-compassion most. Why? Because shame appears precisely in those areas where we've internalized impossible standards or judgments. That uncomfortable feeling is actually showing us where healing is needed, where we need to soften toward ourselves.

Guilt can reveal what we truly value. When we feel guilty, it's because we've acted in a way that conflicts with something we deeply believe in. That discomfort is actually highlighting our core values. If you feel guilty for not calling a friend, for instance, it shows you value connection and reliability.

Heartbreak shows us where we're capable of deep love. The depth of our pain directly reflects the depth of our capacity to care. We only feel heartbroken about things that matter profoundly to us. That ache is evidence of your heart's remarkable ability to connect and care.

Regret highlights what matters most to us. We don't regret things that are unimportant to us. That feeling of "if only" points directly to what we consider truly meaningful in life - whether it's relationships, integrity, courage, or something else entirely. Instead of pushing these emotions away, what if we learned to see them as messengers, bringing important information?

"Emma" - carried deep shame about a business failure, but she didn't even realise it. She hadn't recognised the stories she was telling herself. Emma had founded and run a highly successful fashion retail business for nearly two decades, with multiple shops and a team of 30 at its peak. Over time, her passion for the business dwindled, the retail landscape changed dramatically, and eventually the business folded and she went through insolvency.

For years, she'd tried to bury this chapter of her story, to pretend it hadn't happened. She told herself she was FINE. But when she finally had the courage to look at it directly during our work together, something remarkable happened. Emma discovered that within that "failure" were the seeds of her greatest strengths - resilience, creativity, and a profound compassion for others facing challenges. By reclaiming her whole story, including the difficult parts, Emma found a newfound sense of wholeness. The shame didn't disappear completely, but when she embraced it, it transformed from something that controlled her to something that informed her wisdom.

It takes courage. As Margaret Mead says, sometimes your only form of transportation is a leap of faith. And it has to be a safe space, because there's a lot of trust involved. This isn't about just wearing your heart on your sleeve and babbling out to anybody you meet. That very often can cause more problems than it solves. It's about really knowing, exploring, finding out who you can trust to go deep.

For some, it might need to be a trained trauma practitioner or a specialist in your particular experience. But for most of us, it's about finding someone you trust, who has the ability to hold that space for you, for you to go deep and still be okay. This is not usually a friend or family member because it's often hard to 'come back' from deep sharing, and they can end up (inadvertently and with love) holding you back, keeping you in the place of darkness.

Remember, this is very precious - it's the heart of you, the core of you. So it's very important to find the right person to open up to.

This reminds me of Kintsugi - that beautiful Japanese art of golden repair that we touched on in the last chapter. When pottery breaks, instead of hiding the cracks or throwing it away, artisans repair it with gold. The broken lines become the most valuable, most beautiful part of the piece.

What if we approached our hearts the same way? What if, instead of hiding our wounds or pretending they don't exist, we honoured them as part of what makes us uniquely ourselves?

Nelson Mandela embodied this principle so beautifully. He could have emerged from 27 years in prison bitter and vengeful. No one would have blamed him. But instead, he transformed that experience into something golden - a compassion and vision that helped heal a divided nation.

Your past - with all its joys and sorrows - doesn't define you. But your willingness to embrace it, to learn from it, to find the gold in even the most difficult experiences - that can become your greatest strength.

## The Wisdom of Seven Generations: Your Heart in Context

There's a beautiful concept in Japanese culture of considering seven generations - looking back seven generations to learn from the past, and looking forward seven generations to inspire the future.

This isn't just a philosophical idea. It's a practical approach to understanding our place in the great flow of life. Seven generations represents about 150 years in each direction - connecting us to both our ancestors and those who will inherit what we leave behind.

When we look back seven generations, we begin to see the patterns, beliefs, and experiences that have subtly shaped us. Perhaps your grandmother was taught to keep her feelings private, and her mother before her. Perhaps your great-grandfather lived through war or economic hardship that changed how the family approached security and trust. These experiences don't just disappear - they ripple forward, shaping how love is expressed or withheld, how emotions are honoured or suppressed.

Looking forward seven generations invites us to consider the legacy of our heart work. The forgiveness you practice today doesn't just free you - it might free your children from carrying that same burden. The ways you learn to love more openly might create new possibilities for those who come after you, people you'll never meet but whose lives will be touched by the healing you do now.

I love this way of thinking about our lives, our hearts. We're not isolated beings - we're part of a great flowing river of humanity. The patterns in our hearts often have roots in the past, and the healing we do now creates ripples into the future.

Think about your own family stories. Are there patterns around love, vulnerability, and connection that have been passed down? Perhaps a tendency to keep emotions hidden, or to give endlessly without receiving? Maybe there are beautiful traditions of expressing love that you carry forward, or patterns you're consciously changing?

I worked with a client once who realized she had inherited a belief that showing vulnerability was dangerous. As we explored her family history, she discovered stories of her grandparents surviving extremely difficult circumstances (in Poland) where stoicism was literally a survival skill. What had been adaptive for them had become limiting for her. Understanding this brought her tremendous compassion - both for herself and for those who came before her.

This perspective isn't about blaming the past, but about seeing the bigger picture with kind eyes. It helps us recognize that some of our heart patterns aren't personal failures but inherited ways of being that made sense in their time.

And just as importantly, the heart work you do today isn't just for you. When you learn to love more fully, to forgive, to connect authentically - you create new possibilities that ripple outward. The courage you show in healing your heart might inspire someone seven generations from now in ways you can't even imagine.

What a beautiful thought - that your heart's journey today might be creating space for greater love in the distant future.

# Practical Ways to Open Your Heart

Just as we talked about simple, daily practices for grounding in Chapter 1, here are some gentle ways to work with your Heart Chakra. These aren't complicated techniques - they're more like coming home to your heart:

### 🫳 "The Heart Meditation"

This is perfect with your morning tea or coffee. Place one hand over your heart, feeling its warmth and steady rhythm. Take three deep breaths, imagining with each inhale that you're drawing light and warmth into your heart centre. With each exhale, imagine releasing any protection or tension you've been holding. Just a minute or two of this simple practice can shift your entire day.

### ✍️ "The Gratitude Letter"

This is one of my favourite practices when my heart feels a bit closed or heavy. Take a piece of paper (yes, actual paper rather than typing) and write a letter to someone who has touched your heart. You don't even need to send it - though you certainly can if it feels right. The simple act of acknowledging how someone has impacted you opens channels of love and appreciation.

### 🤍 "The Kitchen-Sink Truth Moment"

Next time you're at your kitchen sink - whether washing dishes, preparing vegetables, or simply filling the kettle - try this: Ask yourself "How am I really doing right now?" Allow whatever arises to simply be there, without judgement. Sometimes just acknowledging our truth - even if only to ourselves, even if only for a moment - creates space for the heart to breathe.

When your heart feels particularly guarded or your emotions overwhelming, here's what helps:

**Get Back to Basics**

- Place your hand on your heart and feel its beat
- Make yourself a nourishing cup of tea or simple meal
- Wrap yourself in something soft and warm
- Connect with nature, even if just looking out your window
- Reach out to someone you trust

**Use Your Senses to Come Home to Your Heart**

Notice:

- What you can see that brings beauty into your day
- What you can touch that feel comforting should be what you can see that brings beauty into your day
- What you can touch that feels comforting
- What you can smell that brings you back to yourself
- What you can taste that reminds you of care and nourishment

This practice goes beyond simple awareness - it's an invitation to return home to yourself, to anchor in the present moment where your heart naturally begins to open and soften.

# Taking a Deeper Look

Let's pause for a moment, just as we might pause between mouthfuls. I've found that thoughtful questions can illuminate corners of ourselves we've never fully explored. Not to search for perfect answers, but to gently deepen our self-understanding.

Here are eight questions to sit with over the coming days, they are also perfect journal prompts:

1. Where in my life am I "guarding my heart"? We all have protective patterns - perhaps in certain relationships, or around specific vulnerabilities. Simply noticing these patterns with compassion is the first step toward choice.

2. What past wounds still affect my ability to "give or receive love"? Old hurts often shape our present connections in ways we don't fully recognise.

3. Who in my life do I need to "forgive, even if it's just for my own peace"? Remember that forgiveness isn't about condoning what happened - it's about freeing yourself from carrying the weight. But the forgiveness needs to be real, you can't fake it.

4. How can I show "more self-love and compassion"? The heart chakra isn't just about loving others - it begins with how we treat ourselves.

5. What relationships bring me "joy, and which ones drain me"? Pay attention to how you feel after spending time with different people in your life.

6. How can I practice "both giving and receiving love more freely"? Many of us excel at one but struggle with the other.

7. What fears about love am I "ready to release"? Our hearts often protect us from old fears that may no longer be relevant. "I'm never going to love again" is a common knee jerk reaction to hurt but what is really under the surface?

8. How can I bring "more kindness and warmth into my daily life"? Sometimes the smallest gestures create the most significant shifts.

These aren't questions to answer all at once. Let them sit with you. Notice what comes up as you go about your day. You might be surprised by what you discover.

Use this space to jot down anything that comes up for you.

## Coming Home to Your Heart

You know how I open my window each night? I never know exactly what I'll experience - sometimes it's mild, other times it's chilly. Sometimes there's rain blowing in, occasionally even snow! But whatever it brings, it's always perfect in that moment.

This is what I've learned about the heart - it's not about experiencing only positive emotions or connections. It's about being open to the full spectrum of what it means to be human. Joy and sorrow. Connection and loneliness. Giving and receiving. All of it has a place.

Building this openness isn't a one-time achievement. It's more like my morning and evening practices - something we return to, day after day. Sometimes it feels natural and easy. Other times we have to remind ourselves to pause, to breathe, to come back to our hearts.

Remember:

- Connection doesn't require perfection - it flourishes in authenticity
- Love isn't just something you give or receive - it's who you are at your core
- Your heart knows how to heal - our job is to create the conditions for that healing
- Small, consistent moments of truth matter more than grand gestures

Before we move on to the next chapter, I invite you to choose one small way to connect with your heart today. Maybe it's placing your hand on your chest and taking three deep breaths when you feel stressed. Perhaps it's speaking one truth you've been holding back. Or simply making yourself to a rose and cardamom tea as an act of self-care.

What matters isn't how big or small the practice is - it's the presence and intention you bring to it.

Are you ready to explore what comes next?

# Recipe: Strawberry Passion!

This playful desert ties in beautifully with the Heart chakra. Strawberries are associated with love and I created this recipe for a Valentine's treat back in 2011.

You've probably never thought of sauteing strawberries but just wait!

## Ingredients

- 1/2 lb/225g strawberries
- ½ oz/14g butter
- Zest of an orange
- Juice of ½ an orange
- 1 tbsp/15ml brandy

## The Practice

1. Saute the strawberries lightly in the butter with the zest of orange.
2. Add the juice and bubble for a few moments to reduce slightly
3. Tip the pan to one side and add the brandy - set it alight with a match (please do be careful not to set anything else alight!)

That's it!

All very quick, delicious and fun to make your heart sing.

A reminder that the companion Workbook to Ellev8 Book One "Letting the Light in" is for sale on Amazon and elsewhere but... I would like to give you a copy of the pdf as a Gift to enhance your whole experience as you go on this journey with me.

You can download it via the QR code or at this link:

https://tinyurl.com/Letting-the-Light-in-Workbook

## Chapter 5
# SPEAKING YOUR TRUTH
*The Throat Chakra, Voice & Expression*

---
*"Your voice matters. The question is — are you using it?"*
---

### Dear Ellev8'ing One,

Have you ever found yourself nodding in agreement when every cell in your body wanted to scream "no"? Or perhaps you've swallowed your words rather than risk making waves, only to lie awake later replaying what you wish you'd said?

I was sitting at my dining table yesterday, sipping tea and watching birds gather at the feeder outside my window. A blue tit landed first, then quickly flew away when larger birds arrived. It made me think about how often we do the same — retreat when louder voices enter the space, even when we have every right to be there.

I was brought up by very loving parents but we were certainly expected to be "good" well behaved children and my grandfather was distinctly Victorian.

For much of my life, I believed that keeping quiet was the kind way, the polite way, the good way to be. What I didn't realise was that each time I muted my truth, I wasn't just being kind to others — I was being unkind to myself - and actually I wasn't really even being kind to them.

This chapter is about reclaiming that voice that has always been within you. Not by becoming someone you're not, but by allowing the true you to be heard — perhaps for the first time in a very long time.

### With love, light and grace
### Karen 🩶 xxx

# The Sound of Silence

Just as we explored how to ground ourselves in Chapter 1, how to flow with life's rhythms in Chapter 2, how to stand in our power in Chapter 3, and how to open our hearts in Chapter 4 — now we're learning to speak our truth. But this isn't about becoming louder or more forceful than everyone else. It's about something far more authentic — finding the clear, honest voice that resonates from your core.

Think about a time when you didn't speak up when something mattered to you. Perhaps it was in a meeting where your idea wasn't acknowledged. Maybe it was in a relationship where your needs went unexpressed. Or perhaps it was simply not telling someone how much they meant to you when you had the chance.

How did that silence feel in your body? For many of us, unexpressed truth sits like a weight in our throat or a tightness in our chest. It takes energy to hold back what needs to be said — energy that could be used for creativity, connection, and joy.

The Throat Chakra, which we'll explore together, is where this voice lives. It's the energy centre that governs:

- 🎤 Your authentic expression (not just words, but your creative voice too)
- 🎤 Your ability to speak your truth (even when it's difficult)
- 🎤 Your capacity to listen deeply (hearing is as important as speaking)

When this energy centre flows freely, you might notice:

- Words come easily when they need to

- You can set boundaries without excessive guilt
- Creative expression feels natural and joyful
- You speak with confidence, even when your voice shakes
- You listen as deeply as you speak

But when it's blocked (and yes, most of us have experienced blocks), you might find:

- Words catching in your throat when you need them most
- Difficulty expressing needs and setting boundaries
- Creative blocks that frustrate your self-expression
- Speaking either too much (to fill silence) or too little (afraid to take space)
- Listening without truly hearing

## Finding Your Voice After Years of Silence

Many of us were taught, in ways both subtle and direct, that our voices weren't worth hearing. Perhaps you heard:

"Children should be seen and not heard." "That's not appropriate for the dinner table." "Nobody wants to hear about that." "Don't be so sensitive." "Stop making such a fuss."

These messages weren't just about specific moments — they taught us to question the value of our perspective entirely. Over time, we learned that safety meant silence, that belonging required blending in, that love was conditional on not rocking the boat.

People use the word 'just' so often, but it is a form of hiding, of diminishing your self. The sad thing is, how often people say, 'it's just me,' when they make a phone call for example. No, no, there is no 'just you.' It's you - all of you.

Then it gets into that whole thing about how we speak to ourselves. We live with that day in day out, minute in minute out. Most of the time, before we start really doing deep work and understanding it, we talk to ourselves in a way we would never dream of talking to someone that we care about.

We're brutal. Saying things like 'you're stupid. Why did you do that?' and beating ourselves up for everything. We wouldn't have any friends if we did that to them. But we wouldn't dream of doing it to our friends. So it is very much about learning to value ourselves, self-love, self-worth, self-value, so that we're not diminishing ourselves and our place in the world.

We all have a valid and important place in the world. And part of this wonderful experiment of being alive and on this earth for however long is finding out exactly what that is. What is our purpose? Why are we here? This is something we are going to come back to.

Think about how we make tea. When water is cold, it's silent. As it begins to warm, small bubbles form but barely make a sound. It's only when it reaches its boiling point that it finds its voice — singing, steaming, impossible to ignore.

People are much the same. We often stay quiet, simmering beneath the surface, until something within us can no longer be contained. But what if we didn't wait for that boiling point? What if we learned to express ourselves clearly before reaching that stage of frustration or despair?

I worked with a client called "Sarah" who came to me feeling depleted and resentful in her relationships. "I give and give," she told me, "but no one seems to notice what I need." As we explored further, a pattern emerged: Sarah had never directly asked for what she needed. She expected others to intuit her desires, then felt hurt when they didn't.

Her first attempts at expressing her needs felt awkward, even selfish to her. "Who am I to ask for what I want?" she wondered. But as she practised, something remarkable happened. Not only did she begin receiving more of what she needed, but her relationships deepened. Her authentic voice created space for authentic connection.

This is what finding your voice is really about — not just speaking up, but speaking from a place of truth that opens the door to genuine understanding and intimacy.

# The Throat Chakra: The Bridge Between Heart and Mind

Remember how we explored the foundation of the Root Chakra, the creative flow of the Sacral Chakra, the personal power of the Solar Plexus Chakra, and the compassion of the Heart Chakra? Well, the Throat Chakra builds on all of these. It sits at the base of your throat — that place that might tighten when you're holding back tears or words.

The ancient teachers called it 'Vishuddha' — which means "especially pure." This name points to something profound: your truest voice comes from a place of clarity and authenticity. Not from ego or reactivity, but from the purest expression of who you are.

In our everyday lives, the Throat Chakra is where:

- Internal knowing transforms into external expression
- Thoughts and feelings find form through words and creative acts
- We bridge the gap between our inner and outer worlds
- We learn to listen as deeply as we speak

When this energy centre is flowing freely, you might notice:

- You can express difficult truths with compassion
- Creative ideas flow more easily into form
- You listen without immediately preparing your response
- Your words align with your actions
- You can both speak up and hold silence when appropriate

But when it's blocked (and these blocks are so common in our culture), you might find:

- Words emerging as either too harsh or too timid
- Creative expression feeling stuck or forced
- Listening without truly hearing
- A gap between what you say and what you do
- Either dominating conversations or fading into the background

## The Balance of Speaking and Listening

True communication isn't just about finding your voice — it's about creating space for authentic exchange. This requires both the courage to speak and the patience to listen. Both are equally sacred parts of expression.

Think about those rare conversations where you feel truly heard. Not just someone waiting for their turn to speak, but actively taking in your words, considering them, responding to what you've actually said rather than what they assume you meant. How precious those moments are! And how rarely they occur in our distracted, fast-paced world.

When I first met my former husband and I was hosting a party he was struck by the level of attention my friends all paid when someone else was speaking. They were all totally present. It is not the norm - hence him commenting.

This balance between speaking and listening reflects the Ellev8 philosophy we explored in Chapter 2 — the continuous flow between masculine and feminine energies that exists within each of us:

The masculine energy gives us the courage to assert our voice, to stand firm in our truth. The feminine energy gives us the openness to truly listen, to receive others' truths without immediately judging or responding. Neither is more important than the other. In fact, they enhance each other. Our speaking becomes more powerful when we've truly listened. Our listening becomes more profound when we honour our own voice as well.

I remember sitting across from my mother during a difficult conversation. For years, certain topics had been off-limits, creating an invisible wall between us. That day, I found the courage to speak a truth I'd held back for decades. But what happened next surprised me even more than my own courage: she listened. Really listened. Not with defence or a need to explain, but with an open heart.

Both acts — my speaking and her listening — required bravery. Both were acts of love. And in that exchange, something that had been frozen for years began to thaw.

## When Speaking Is Hard: Finding Your Voice

If you've spent years keeping quiet, finding your voice might feel overwhelming. Where do you even begin? How do you express what's been silent for so long?

Here are some gentle practices that have helped my clients (and myself) strengthen the Throat Chakra:

### 🗣 Morning Voice Practice

Before checking your phone or speaking to anyone else, take a moment to greet yourself. It might sound something like: "Good morning. What's true for me today is..." This simple practice acknowledges your voice as the first one that matters each day.

### 📝 The Unsent Letter

When something feels too difficult to say directly, write it down as a letter you don't intend to send. This allows your voice to flow without the immediate pressure of response. Sometimes, just seeing your truth on paper helps clarify what actually needs to be communicated.

### 🎵 Sound as Medicine

Humming, singing, or even just making gentle sounds while you breathe can help release tension in the throat. Try humming while preparing your morning tea, or singing along to a favourite song when driving alone. These simple acts remind your body that it's safe to make sound, to take up audible space in the world.

But what about when speaking up feels not just difficult, but frightening? When you worry about rejection, conflict, or consequences?

**When Fear Blocks Your Voice:**
- Start with writing to clarify what you truly want to express
- Practise with someone safe before having difficult conversations
- Remember that speaking up might feel selfish but is actually a gift of truth
- Focus on "I" statements rather than accusations
- Give yourself permission for imperfect expression

**The Power of "I" Statements:**

Rather than: "You never listen to me." Try: "I feel unheard when my ideas aren't acknowledged."

Rather than: "You're always late." Try: "I feel anxious when plans change without notice."

Rather than: "You should know what I want." Try: "I need to be more clear about what matters to me."

These aren't just communication techniques — they're ways of honouring both your truth and the dignity of the person you're speaking with. They create bridges rather than walls.

# The Art of Saying No: Boundaries and Truth

One of the most powerful words in the English language is also one of the shortest: "No."

For many of us, especially women, saying no can feel almost impossible. We've been conditioned to prioritise others' comfort over our own needs, to be available always, to say yes even when our bodies and spirits are screaming no.

But here's a truth I've learned: saying no to what doesn't align with your values is saying yes to what does. Every time you decline something that drains you, you create space for what nourishes you.

A client once told me about attending her monthly book club. "I dread it," she admitted. "I never enjoy the books, the conversation is shallow, and I leave feeling depleted." When I asked why she continued to go, she looked surprised. "I never considered that I could just... stop." For a fun and clever take on this watch Bob Newhart's brilliant sketch "Stop it" which you can find on YouTube - it will stay with you!

But that's exactly it — we always have the choice to say no, even to things we've said yes to for years. Even to things that look good on paper. Even to things that others expect from us.

Learning to say no isn't selfish — it's self-honouring. It acknowledges that your time and energy are precious resources that deserve to be spent in alignment with what truly matters to you.

Some gentle ways to strengthen your "no" muscle:

- Start with smaller nos before tackling bigger ones
- Buy yourself time with "Let me think about that and get back to you"
- Remember that "No" is a complete sentence (though you can certainly elaborate if you choose)
- Practise in the mirror if saying no feels particularly challenging
- Celebrate each no as an act of self-respect, not rejection of others

What might change in your life if you said no to what depletes you and yes to what energises you? What boundaries have you been afraid to set that, if established, might actually lead to healthier relationships? Learning to say no allows us to say yes to more of what we really want.

## The Conviction Gap: Finding Your Confidence

Have you noticed how some people speak with such certainty, even when they're not particularly knowledgeable on a topic? Meanwhile, true experts often hedge their statements with qualifiers and uncertainties.

Studies have found a fascinating pattern: men will typically apply for jobs when they meet just 60% of the qualifications, while women often wait until they meet 100% before applying. This same pattern extends to how we express ourselves — men generally speak with more conviction, even with less expertise, while women tend to qualify their statements even when highly knowledgeable.

This isn't about gender stereotyping, but rather recognising patterns created by how different genders are socialised. From childhood, boys are often encouraged to take risks and assert themselves, while girls are frequently rewarded for being accommodating and perfect.

The result? A conviction gap that affects how confidently we express our truth.

Think about your own patterns:

- Do you use qualifiers like "just," "sort of," "kind of," "maybe," or "I think" when stating your position?
- Do you phrase statements as questions with an upward intonation?
- Do you apologise before expressing your thoughts?
- Do you wait until you're 100% certain before speaking up?

None of these patterns make your voice less valuable — but they might make it less heard. Learning to speak with conviction doesn't mean becoming someone you're not. It means allowing your truth to emerge without the filters of doubt and apology that often dilute it.

Try this: Next time you're about to share an idea or opinion, take a deep breath and remove just one qualifier. Instead of "I just wanted to suggest that maybe we could try..." try "I suggest we try..." Notice how different that feels in your body. I'm willing to bet there's a bit of superhero energy about you!

True conviction doesn't come from bravado or performance. It emerges naturally when you're aligned with your truth and speaking from that centred place within.

# Women Who Spoke Anyway: Finding Inspiration

Throughout history, women have been told in countless ways that their voices don't matter. Yet many spoke anyway, often at great personal cost, changing the course of history with their courage.

Consider these women who refused to be silenced:

**Rosa Parks** didn't give a lengthy speech when she refused to give up her seat on that Montgomery bus in 1955. Her power came in a simple, firm "No." That single word, backed by conviction, helped launch a movement that transformed a nation.

**Malala Yousafzai** was shot by the Taliban for advocating for girls' education in Pakistan. After surviving, she said, "They thought that the bullets would silence us, but they failed." Today, her voice reaches millions around the world.

**Ruth Bader Ginsburg** was told she shouldn't take a man's place at law school, despite graduating top of her class. Years later, as a Supreme Court Justice, she said: "Women belong in all places where decisions are being made... It shouldn't be that women are the exception."

These women didn't speak up because it was easy or safe. They spoke because remaining silent would have been a betrayal of their truth. Their courage doesn't mean they weren't afraid — it means they spoke anyway.

What truth within you is waiting to be expressed? What might change if you allowed that voice to be heard?

# The Power of Words: Creation or Destruction

Words hold incredible power. They can heal or hurt, build or break, empower or diminish.

Think about the last time someone's words lifted you up. Perhaps someone acknowledged a quality in you that you value but rarely hear recognised. Maybe someone expressed genuine appreciation for something you did. How did those words affect not just your mood, but your sense of what's possible for you?

Now think about words that have cut you down. The criticism that wasn't constructive but crushing. The offhand comment that stayed with you for years. The label that became a limitation. Unfortunately criticism tends to stay with us way longer than praise.

Words create worlds — both within us and around us.

This isn't just poetic language. Neuroscience shows that our brains physically respond to words. Negative words release stress hormones and can activate our fear response. Positive, encouraging words can stimulate the brain's reward centres and even strengthen neural connections associated with well-being.

The words we speak to others matter deeply. But perhaps even more powerful are the words we speak to ourselves.

What stories do you tell yourself about who you are and what's possible for you? What words do you use when you make a mistake? How do you narrate your own life?

If you find your self-talk is harsh or limiting, try this simple practice: Speak to yourself as you would to a beloved friend. Use the same tone, the same compassion, the same encouragement you would naturally offer someone you care about deeply.

This isn't about fake positivity or denying genuine challenges. It's about treating yourself with the same kindness and respect you would show to someone you love. Because how can we speak our truth to the world if we're not first truthful and kind with ourselves?

## Taking a Deeper Look

Let's pause for a moment, just as we might pause between sips of tea. As mentioned in previous chapters, I've found that thoughtful questions can illuminate corners of ourselves we've never fully explored. Not to search for perfect answers, but to gently deepen our self-understanding.

Think about...

1. Where in your life are you holding back your voice? Notice the situations or relationships where you tend to silence yourself. What patterns do you see?

2. What happens in your body when you don't speak your truth? Perhaps tension in your throat, tightness in your chest, or a knot in your stomach. Your body often signals when your voice needs expression.

3. What old messages about your voice still influence you? Many of us carry childhood directives like "be quiet," "don't make a scene," or "that's not appropriate."

4. When do you feel most comfortable expressing yourself? With certain people? In specific environments? What creates that sense of safety?

5. How do you respond to others' truths, especially when they differ from yours? Our ability to hear others often reflects our relationship with our own voice.

6. What creative expression calls to you? Your voice isn't just about words — it might emerge through art, music, movement, cooking, gardening, or countless other forms.

7. What truth have you been afraid to acknowledge, even to yourself? Sometimes our most important truths are the ones we've hidden from our own awareness.

8. What is one small step you could take today to honour your voice? Remember that reclaiming your expression doesn't have to happen all at once — small, consistent steps create lasting change.

These aren't questions to answer all at once. Let them sit with you. Notice what emerges as you go about your day. You might be surprised by what reveals itself when you create space for your truth to emerge.

Use this space to jot down anything that comes up for you.

# The Truth Meditation: A Daily Practice

Here is a simple meditation you can practise daily to strengthen your connection with your authentic voice. This works beautifully after your morning tea or coffee, or whenever you need to reconnect with your truth.

1. Find a comfortable seated position, either on a chair or cushion.
2. Place one hand gently on your throat and the other on your heart.
3. Take three deep breaths, feeling the connection between these two centres.
4. Ask yourself: "What truth needs expression today?"
5. Don't rush to answer. Allow words, images, or sensations to arise naturally.
6. Notice what emerges without judgement or analysis.
7. When you're ready, thank yourself for this moment of honesty.
8. Close by setting an intention for how you'll honour your voice today.

This practice takes just 2-3 minutes, but it creates a powerful connection with your authentic expression. Like checking in with a dear friend, it maintains the relationship with your own voice.

## Coming Home to Your Voice

You know in the evenings when I open my window to greet the night sky? Sometimes I speak to the stars, sharing thoughts I haven't voiced elsewhere. There's something about that vast, accepting darkness that makes truth-telling easier. Perhaps it's the reminder that my words, like stars, need space to shine (although that sounds a little fanciful).

This is what I've learned about expression — it's not about having the perfect words or the most eloquent delivery. It's about allowing what's true within you to find its way out into the world, in whatever form feels most natural. This is as true of written words as it is about spoken.

Building this authentic expression isn't a one-time achievement. It's more like my morning and evening practices — something we return to, day after day. Sometimes our voice flows easily. Other times we have to gently coax it out of hiding. Either way, the practice of speaking our truth becomes easier with time and compassion.

Remember:

- Your voice matters, not because it's perfect, but because it's yours
- Expression includes both speaking and listening
- Your creative voice is as important as your spoken one
- Small truths spoken consistently create more change than grand statements rarely make

Before we move on to the next chapter, I invite you to choose one small way to honour your voice today. Maybe it's speaking up in a meeting when you'd normally stay silent. Perhaps it's writing down a truth you've been avoiding. Or humming while you prepare dinner, reminding your body of its natural capacity for sound and expression.

What matters isn't how big or dramatic your expression is — it's the authenticity you bring to it.

Are you ready to explore what comes next?

# Recipe: Mouth Watering Tartiflette!

There's something about the smell of tartiflette cooking, and then the taste, that makes your mouth water and you find yourself going "mmmmmm" in anticipation! It's comfort food yes. But there's an honesty about a few ingredients coming together to create such magic.

## Ingredients

- 1kg (2lb 4oz) waxy potatoes, peeled
- 100g (3½oz) (min!) bacon lardons or chopped rashers
- 1 onion, sliced
- 1 or 2 cloves garlic, peeled and sliced
- A little butter
- 100g (3½oz) Emmenthal grated
- 230-250g (8-9oz) whole Rebluchon cheese, sliced
- Black pepper
- Small glass white wine (about 125ml or 4 fl oz)
- 200ml (7 fl oz) double cream

## The Practice

1. Heat the oven to 180°C (350°F/Gas Mark 4)
2. Cook the potatoes in boiling water for 10-15 minutes depending on size until just soft but holding their shape. Set them aside to cool.
3. While potatoes are cooking saute the bacon, onion and garlic together until softened and golden brown.

4. Pour in the white wine - stir to deglaze the pan and allow to bubble and reduce to half the quantity.
5. Thinly slice the potatoes.
6. Butter a casserole dish
7. Layer as follows: potato, bacon mix, potato, emmenthal, potato, bacon mix, potato. Seasoning with a little cracked black pepper on some of the layers.
8. Pour the cream over the top then cover the top with Rebluchon.
9. Bake for about 40 minutes until cooked through (it should be really soft), golden brown and with edges becoming crunchy.

Enjoy! I'm hungry now! Mmmmmm……

## Chapter 6
# SEEING CLEARLY
*The Third Eye Chakra, Intuition & Inner Vision*

---
*"You already know the answer. The question is—
are you willing to trust yourself?"*

---

### Dear Ellev8'ing One,

Have you ever had that feeling? That quiet knowing that whispers to you before logic has a chance to speak? Perhaps it was about a person you'd just met, a decision that seemed right on paper but felt wrong in your body, a potential home you were viewing, or a path that called to you even when others couldn't understand why.

I was standing at my kitchen window this morning, watching the first light touch the hills. There was a moment—brief but profound—where everything seemed perfectly clear. Not because I had all the answers, but because I suddenly trusted the questions.

This is the gift of inner vision—not some mystical superpower, but that deep knowing we all carry within us. That wisdom that's often drowned out by the noise of should's and expectations and endless second opinions.

For much of my life, I believed that answers came from outside myself—from experts, from books, from those who seemed more qualified to guide my path. What I didn't realise was that while external knowledge has its place, my deepest guidance system had been within me all along.

This chapter is about reclaiming that inner vision that has always been your birthright. Not by becoming someone you're not, but by remembering who you've always been beneath the layers of doubt and conditioning.

### With love, light and grace

### Karen 🖤 xxx

# Checking Your Vitals: The Pulse of Your Life

Just as we explored grounding in Chapter 1, creative flow in Chapter 2, personal power in Chapter 3, heart-centreed connection in Chapter 4, and authentic expression in Chapter 5—now we're exploring that subtle inner knowing that guides it all.

Think of this chapter as a gentle check-in, like the way you might pause to feel your pulse after climbing a hill. What's the current rhythm of your life? Are you racing so fast that you can't hear your own wisdom? Or perhaps moving so slowly that you've lost connection with your vision?

I like to think of the Third Eye Chakra as the lighthouse of your energy system. Located at the centre of your forehead, just between your eyebrows, it's where:

- Your intuition speaks to you (in whispers, not shouts)
- Your inner vision forms (beyond what physical eyes can see)
- Your clarity emerges (when you're willing to trust it)

When this energy centre flows freely, you might notice:

- Decisions come with ease, even without all the information
- You feel connected to a sense of purpose and direction
- Creative solutions appear seemingly out of nowhere
- You can distinguish between fear-based thinking and genuine intuition
- Life feels more like a dance and less like a battle

But when it's blocked (as many of us experience in our logic-driven world), you might find:

- Constant overthinking and analysis paralysis
- Difficulty trusting yourself without external validation
- A foggy sense of purpose or direction
- Overreliance on others' opinions
- A disconnect between what you "know" and what you "feel"

Think of a time when you knew something without knowing how you knew it. Perhaps you had a sudden urge to call someone who, it turned out, needed to hear from you right then. Maybe you felt compelled to take a different route home and avoided an accident. Or perhaps you just had a clear sense about a decision that later proved exactly right.

Those moments weren't random luck—they were glimpses of your inner vision at work.

I had a powerful experience of this when I was living in Hampstead London. I was going for a walk and headed for Hampstead Heath - a large and lovely area popular with walkers - but my body screamed no. As I got closer it got louder. So, I didn't go onto the Heath, I walked elsewhere. Later I learnt that a woman had been seriously sexually abused on the Heath that afternoon - in the same area and at the exact time that I would have been there. You can imagine how grateful I was that I had listened to my inner knowing.

We need to disconnect from the outside to connect to the inside. Our connection on the inside actually tells us what we're going to see on the outside. So everything outside is purely a reflection. The same scenario can be going on outside - your financial situation, relationships, business, home can all be the same. But we can have a completely different perception if we disconnect, come inside, really connect, and then view it with effectively different eyes.

## The Third Eye Chakra: Your Inner Compass

The ancient teachers called this energy centre 'Ajna'—which means "to perceive" or "to command." This beautiful name captures something vital: true seeing isn't passive. It's an active engagement with both inner and outer reality, where perception becomes a kind of gentle command over your path.

In our everyday lives, the Third Eye Chakra is where:

- Intuition speaks before logic has assembled all the facts
- Creative visions form before they become physical reality
- Truth is recognised beyond what is immediately apparent
- Alignment with purpose becomes clear

When this energy centre is flowing freely, you might notice:

- An ability to sense what's right for you without excessive deliberation
- Flashes of insight or creative inspiration that seem to arrive fully formed
- A natural ability to read situations and people accurately
- Dreams that offer meaningful guidance
- Trust in the unfolding of your path, even when you can't see the entire journey

But when it's blocked (and our analytical culture often creates these blocks), you might find:

- Confusion about your path or purpose

- Difficulty making decisions without seeking multiple opinions
- Dismissing your hunches, only to discover later they were correct
- Insomnia or restless dreams that don't feel restorative
- Feeling lost or disconnected from your inner guidance

The beautiful paradox of the Third Eye Chakra is that while it deals with vision, its wisdom often arrives through other senses—a feeling in your body, a sudden knowing, a persistent thought that won't let go. Learning to recognise and trust these signals is the art of developing your inner vision.

## The Balance of Intuition and Analysis

One of the most powerful insights I've gained in my work is this: intuition and analysis aren't opposed—they're dance partners. True wisdom emerges when we honour both our inner knowing and our capacity for thoughtful evaluation.

Think about baking bread. There's science to it—precise measurements, chemical reactions, temperature control. But any experienced baker will tell you that knowing when the dough feels right, when the bread is perfectly baked, comes from a place beyond recipes. It's a knowing in the hands, in the nose, in that sense that says "now" before the timer rings.

That's how life works too. We need both the recipe (the structure, the analysis, the plan) and the intuitive knowing that guides us beyond what any formula can provide.

This balance is at the heart of the Ellev8 philosophy we've been exploring throughout this book:

The masculine energy gives us the focus, the structure, the analytical tools to evaluate options. The feminine energy gives us intuition, receptivity, and that inner knowing that speaks before evidence appears. Neither is complete without the other. When they work together, that's when magic happens.

One of my clients—let's call her Jane - came to me feeling completely stuck in her career. On paper, she had an impressive job with a prestigious company. She'd ticked all the boxes she thought she should tick. Yet something felt profoundly wrong.

"Everyone tells me I should be grateful," she told me. "And logically, I know they're right. But something in me knows this isn't where I'm meant to be."

As we worked together, Jane began to honour both aspects of her wisdom—the practical awareness of what her job provided (security, status, certain skills) and her intuitive knowing that her true path lay elsewhere. Not by impulsively quitting, but by gradually creating space to explore what truly called to her while still meeting her practical needs.

Within a year, she had transitioned to a role that felt aligned with both her values and her vision. The key wasn't choosing intuition over analysis, but learning to let them inform each other.

## Eight Vital Areas:
## Checking the Pulse of Your Life

Just as a doctor checks multiple vital signs to assess overall health, we can look at eight essential areas of life to check our alignment with our inner vision. Remember, this isn't about scoring yourself or finding fault—it's about honest awareness, the starting point for any meaningful change.

Take a moment to consider each area, noticing both how you're doing structurally (the practical aspects) and intuitively (how it feels in your being):

1. **Work & Purpose Structure:** Do you have clear goals? Are you productive and focused? **Intuition**: Does your work feel meaningful? Are you energised or drained by it?
2. **Family & Home Structure:** Are your relationships stable? Do you have healthy boundaries? **Intuition**: Does your home feel like a sanctuary? Do family connections nourish you?
3. **Financial Wellbeing Structure:** Are you meeting your practical needs? Saving for the future? **Intuition:** What's your relationship with money? Does it flow or feel constricted?
4. **Spiritual Connection Structure:** Do you have practices that support your spiritual growth? **Intuition:** Do you feel connected to something larger than yourself?
5. **Adventure & Play Structure:** Do you make time for activities that bring joy and expansion? **Intuition:** Does your life feel spacious enough for spontaneity and wonder?
6. **Health & Vitality Structure:** Are you supporting your body's basic needs for movement, nutrition, rest? **Intuition:** Do you feel at home in your body? Do you listen to its wisdom?
7. **Impact & Contribution Structure:** Are you using your gifts in service to something meaningful? **Intuition:** Does your contribution feel aligned with your values and vision?

8. **Relationships & Connection Structure:** Do you nurture important relationships consistently? **Intuition:** Do your connections feel authentic and life-giving?

As you reflect on these areas, you might notice patterns. Perhaps some areas feel structurally solid but intuitively lacking. Others might feel intuitively aligned but needing more practical support.

This balance—between structure and intuition, between doing and being—is the heart of living with clear vision. It's not about perfection in every area, but about honest awareness and gentle alignment.

The question isn't "Am I doing everything right?" but rather "Am I seeing clearly, and am I willing to adjust course based on what I see?"

# Trusting Your Knowing: When Inner Vision Speaks

We all have stories about times we didn't listen to our intuition—and regretted it later. That relationship we stayed in too long despite the warning signs. The job we took even though something felt off during the interview. The decision we made based entirely on others' advice, even as something in us whispered "no."

But what about the times you did listen? What happened when you trusted that quiet voice within?

I worked with a client— "Davina"—who had been offered a significant promotion. On paper, it was exactly what she'd been working toward for years. The title, the salary, the recognition—all the external markers of success.

But something didn't feel right. "It's probably just impostor syndrome," she told me. "I should just push through it."

As we explored deeper, though, it became clear that her intuition was flagging something important. The new role would require her to compromise on values that were essential to her sense of purpose. Her inner vision was seeing something her excitement about the promotion had initially obscured.

Davina ultimately declined the promotion—a decision that seemed baffling to many of her colleagues. Six months later, serious ethical issues emerged in the department she would have led. By trusting her intuition, she had protected not just her integrity but potentially her entire career.

This pattern appears across countless areas of life. Inner knowing often perceives what isn't yet visible to our analytical mind or to external observation.

The challenge for many of us isn't that we lack intuition—it's that we've been taught to distrust it. We live in a world that values data over feeling, proof over perception, external validation over internal knowing. It is also true that in the past (thankfully for most of us although still current for some) those of us using our intuition and "magic" were hunted and killed as witches. That wound is still in us - but we'll explore that another time.

Breaking free from this conditioning begins with simple acknowledgment—recognising that your intuition is already speaking to you, has always been speaking to you, deserves your attention and that it is safe for you to listen to.

# Practical Ways to Strengthen Your Inner Vision

Just as we've explored practical ways to work with each chakra, here are some gentle approaches to strengthen your connection with your inner vision. These aren't complicated techniques—they're simple practices that create space for your intuition to speak:

### 👁 The Morning Question

Before checking your phone or getting caught in the day's demands, take a quiet moment with your morning tea or coffee. Ask yourself: "What do I need to know today?" Then simply listen. The answer might come as a word, an image, a feeling, or simply a sense of knowing. Don't analyze it—just receive it and carry it with you. And don't worry if nothing comes, that's OK too - don't force it. Stay relaxed and unattached to the outcome.

### 👁 The Intuition Tracker

This simple practice helps you recognise how often your intuition is already guiding you correctly. Keep a small notebook handy. Whenever you have a hunch or gut feeling about something, jot it down. Later, when you have more information, note what actually happened. Over time, patterns emerge that help you distinguish between fear-based thinking and genuine intuition.

### ◉ The Body Compass

Your body often registers intuitive knowing before your mind can articulate it. When facing a decision, pause and notice: Does this option create expansion or contraction in your body? Does your breath deepen or become shallow? Does your energy rise or fall? Your body rarely lies about what's aligned for you.

When confusion clouds your vision or decisions feel particularly challenging, try this:

**The Clarity Practice**

- Find a quiet space where you won't be disturbed
- Place both hands over your heart
- Take three deep breaths, longer on the exhale
- Ask your question clearly, then drop it
- For the next few minutes, simply sit in receptive silence
- Notice what arises without grasping or judging it
- Return to your day, allowing insights to emerge in their own time

Remember, clarity rarely comes from forcing answers. Like trying to see stars by staring directly at them, sometimes intuition becomes clearer when you look slightly away, creating space for it to emerge in its own way, in its own time.

# The Soul Questions: Seeing Beyond Surface

In moments of quiet contemplation—perhaps while sipping tea and watching the world from your window—certain questions can help part the veil between everyday awareness and deeper knowing. These aren't questions to answer quickly with your analytical mind, but invitations to listen at a deeper level.

Here are eight soul questions to sit with:

1. What do I know in my bones, even without evidence or approval? Deep knowing often precedes external confirmation.
2. Where am I waiting for permission instead of trusting my vision? We often delay action while waiting for external validation.
3. What recurring dreams or ideas keep visiting me, even when I try to dismiss them? Persistent messages are often your intuition's way of getting your attention.
4. If I already trusted myself completely, what would I do differently? This question bypasses doubt to reveal your clearest vision.
5. What do I sense is coming in my life that I haven't fully acknowledged? Intuition often perceives approaching changes before they become obvious.
6. When do I feel most aligned and clear? What creates that state for me? These patterns reveal when your inner vision functions most naturally.
7. What truth have I been avoiding seeing clearly? Sometimes our biggest insights are the ones we've been avoiding.
8. If my wisest self were to offer me guidance right now, what would it be? This creates space for your highest wisdom to emerge.

These questions aren't meant to be answered all at once. Choose one that resonates, then carry it with you. Let it simmer in the background of your awareness. Notice what bubbles up when you're not trying to force an answer.

The most profound insights often arrive not when we're straining to find them, but when we've created space for them to find us.

## Women Who Trusted Their Vision: Finding Inspiration

Throughout history, women's intuition has often been dismissed or trivialised. Yet many remarkable women have demonstrated the power of trusting inner vision, even when it contradicted conventional wisdom or invited ridicule.

**Jane Goodall** took an approach to studying chimpanzees that defied scientific convention—giving them names instead of numbers, recognising their individual personalities, and forming relationships with them. Her intuitive approach led to revolutionary discoveries that transformed our understanding of both chimpanzees and ourselves.

**Florence Nightingale** revolutionised nursing against immense resistance. Beyond her analytical brilliance with statistics, she trusted her intuitive understanding of what created healing environments. When she insisted on fresh air, nutrition, and emotional support alongside medical treatment, she was following an inner vision of healthcare that has since been validated by research.

**Harriet Tubman**, who led over 300 enslaved people to freedom along the Underground Railroad, repeatedly attributed her success to following her intuition and visions. "I never ran my train off the track," she said, "and I never lost a passenger." Her inner guidance system literally saved lives.

These women didn't separate their analytical capabilities from their intuitive knowing—they integrated them. They demonstrate what becomes possible when we trust our whole way of knowing, not just the parts our culture deems "rational" or "provable."

What might happen if you trusted your inner vision with similar courage?

## Seeing Through Illusion: What's Really True?

One of the most valuable functions of the Third Eye Chakra is its ability to see through illusions—the stories, beliefs, and conditioning that obscure our clearest vision.

Think about how often we mistake these for absolute truth:

- Cultural messaging about what success looks like
- Family beliefs about what's possible or appropriate
- Media images of what happiness requires
- Professional norms about the "right" career path
- Social expectations about how relationships should unfold

Your inner vision allows you to question these assumptions, to ask: "Is this really true for me? Or am I living someone else's version of truth?"

I worked with a client—let's call her Sophia—who had built her entire career around a definition of success she'd inherited from her father. On paper, she'd achieved everything: prestigious position, financial security, professional recognition. But she felt hollow, like she was living someone else's life.

Our work together involved separating her genuine values and vision from those she'd absorbed without questioning. It wasn't easy. Illusions can be comfortable precisely because they're familiar and socially reinforced.

Gradually, though, Sophia began to see clearly what was truly important to her—meaningful connection, creative expression, service to causes she genuinely cared about. As her vision cleared, she didn't abandon her career entirely, but reshaped it to align with her authentic values rather than inherited ones.

Seeing through illusion isn't about rejecting everything you've been taught. It's about conscious discernment—choosing what serves your truest path rather than blindly accepting what you've absorbed.

Ask yourself: What stories have I accepted as "just the way things are" that might actually be limiting illusions? What might become possible if I saw beyond them?

# Taking a Deeper Look

As we've done in previous chapters, let's pause for reflection. These questions invite you to explore your relationship with your inner vision and intuitive wisdom:

**Think about...**

1. When have you experienced moments of absolute clarity? What conditions created that clear seeing? What can you learn from those experiences?

2. Which of the eight vital areas feels most aligned right now? Which feels most in need of attention? Notice where your energy naturally flows and where it feels blocked.

3. What practices help you distinguish between fear-based thinking and genuine intuition? We all have both, and learning to tell the difference is a lifelong practice.

4. Where might you be overvaluing external opinions while undervaluing your own knowing? This pattern often reveals where we've been conditioned to doubt ourselves.

5. What recurring message has your intuition been sending that you've been ignoring? Often we already know what needs attention, even if we've been avoiding it.

6. How do you experience intuitive knowing in your body? Some people feel it as warmth, others as a sense of expansion, others as a quiet certainty. What are your physical signals?

7. What vision for your life keeps returning, even when you try to dismiss it as impractical? Persistent visions often point toward your truest path.

8. What one small step could you take today to honour your inner knowing? Remember that reclaiming your intuitive wisdom happens one choice at a time.

Let these questions sit with you like tea steeping. Don't rush to answer them all at once. Notice what emerges in quiet moments, perhaps when you're at your window watching the day unfold, or when you're engaged in simple, meditative activities like preparing food or walking.

Use this space to jot down anything that comes up for you.

# Coming Home to Your Inner Vision

You know when I open my window wide to the night sky? Sometimes the stars are hidden by clouds, other times they shine with remarkable clarity. But they're always there, whether I can see them or not.

Your intuition is much the same—always present, always offering guidance, even when clouds of doubt or distraction temporarily obscure it. The practice isn't about creating inner vision, but about removing what blocks its natural function.

Developing this relationship with your intuition isn't a one-time achievement. It's more like my morning and evening window rituals—something we return to, day after day. Sometimes clarity comes easily. Other times we need to be patient, trusting that vision will clear in its own time.

**Remember:**

- Your intuition speaks in whispers, not shouts
- Inner knowing often arrives in unexpected ways—feelings, images, persistent thoughts
- The body's wisdom is a profound part of intuitive knowing
- Small moments of trusting yourself build the foundation for deeper vision

Before we move on to the next chapter, I invite you to choose one small way to honour your inner vision today. Perhaps it's taking a moment of stillness before making a decision. Maybe it's finally acknowledging a truth you've been avoiding. Or simply creating a few minutes of quiet space where intuition can speak without the noise of constant doing.

What matters isn't how dramatic your practice is—it's the consistency with which you create space for your own inner wisdom to emerge.

Are you ready to explore what comes next?

# Recipe: Green Goddess Salad

There are many versions of this, this is mine - it is simple and utterly delicious. This is for one beautiful Goddess - you.

## Ingredients

- ¼ little gem lettuce, chopped
- ½ stalk celery, chopped
- 1 spring onion, chopped
- ½ ripe avocado, chopped
- Sea salt
- Cracked black pepper
- Juice ½ lemon
- Drizzle avocado oil
- Handful pumpkin seeds

## The Practice

Toss everything except the seeds together and then sprinkle on the seeds

Give thanks before eating. Feel this nourishing you and aiding your connection with all that is.

## Chapter 7
# RISING ABOVE

*The Crown Chakra, Higher Purpose & Divine Connection*

*"You are part of something greater. The question is—are you ready to receive it?"*

### *Dear Ellev8'ing One,*

Have you ever had that strange feeling of repeating patterns you swore you'd never repeat? Perhaps you heard your parent's exact words come out of your mouth during a moment of stress. Maybe you recognised a familiar dynamic playing out in your relationships. Or perhaps you've caught yourself making the same choices that once frustrated you when you observed them in others.

I was sitting in the lounge yesterday, sorting through old family photographs. There was one that particularly caught my eye—my mother at about my current age, with the same expression I sometimes catch in my own reflection. It made me wonder: How much of who I am was consciously chosen, and how much was simply inherited like eye colour or the shape of my hands?

This is one of life's most profound questions. Which parts of ourselves are truly our own, and which are patterns we've absorbed from family, culture, and experience? More importantly, once we recognise these patterns, how do we consciously choose which to keep and which to transform?

This chapter is about rising above—not in the sense of superiority or escape, but in gaining the perspective that allows for genuine choice. When we can see the patterns that have shaped us, we become free to choose our path rather than unconsciously walking one that was laid out before we were born.

### *With love, light and grace*
### *Karen* 🩶 *xxx*

# The Patterns We Inherit: Seeing with Clear Eyes

Just as we've explored grounding in Chapter 1, creative flow in Chapter 2, personal power in Chapter 3, heart-centred connection in Chapter 4, authentic expression in Chapter 5, and inner vision in Chapter 6—now we're exploring how all of these come together in our connection to something greater than ourselves.

**Think about your most deeply held beliefs about:**

- What it means to be successful
- How love should be expressed (or contained)
- Your relationship with money and security
- Your worth as a human being
- Your relationship with the divine or spiritual realms

How many of these beliefs did you consciously choose? How many were simply absorbed from your family, your culture, your early experiences?

I've been on a personal development, spiritual development journey for over 20 years now. It started when I was in a relationship I was struggling with. I went to a life coach, who sent me to Tony Robbins' UPW weekend. I then signed up for his entire Mastery University programme. But I got to the end, and I knew I hadn't found what my heart and soul were looking for.

At a YES group meeting, I met a man called Babu who was talking in riddles. Somehow, my friend and I found ourselves on a workshop in Capri ten days later, having paid a considerable amount of money! After that workshop, I found myself 'reborn' for want of a different phrase. I think potentially we can be reborn many, many times, and it doesn't have to be religious. I was skipping around the streets of Capri singing - it wasn't religious, but it was definitely spiritual.

I have continued to do work on myself, with that same mentor, with other coaches and mentors, and sometimes on my own. I think we do need some kind of practice, and very often we need someone to help us see what we can't necessarily see on our own.

I'm not suggesting these inherited patterns are wrong or harmful—many are beautiful gifts passed through generations. But there's profound power in distinguishing between what we've chosen and what we've inherited without question.

**The Crown Chakra, which we'll explore together, is located at the top of your head. It's the energy centre that governs:**

- Your connection to something greater than yourself
- Your sense of meaning and purpose beyond the material
- Your ability to transcend limiting patterns and beliefs

**When this energy centre flows freely, you might notice:**

- A sense of being guided by something greater than your personal will
- Peace that persists even during challenging circumstances
- The ability to see patterns in your life from a higher perspective
- Trust in life's unfolding, even when the path isn't clear
- Connection to purpose that transcends personal achievement

**But when it's blocked (as many experience in our achievement-oriented world), you might find:**

- Feeling isolated and solely responsible for everything in your life
- Persistent anxiety and the need to control outcomes
- Difficulty seeing beyond immediate problems to larger patterns
- Spiritual disconnection or emptiness
- A sense that life lacks deeper meaning or purpose

Interestingly, prior to doing this work, people had always said, 'you're such a positive person' or 'the most positive person I've ever known.' And I was - things would happen, because things happen to all of us in life, and I would pick myself up, dust myself down, and carry on, never giving myself time to really explore what had happened, how it had impacted me. So after a period of time, I would burn out.

Eventually it was so severe that I had a nervous breakdown. That was huge learning for me in terms of not ignoring what is going on. Not going 'la la la la la, everything's okay,' when everything's not okay. Allowing myself to go deep into the feelings that are coming up, and really exploring what's underneath.

It's always 'so what's under that, what's under that, what's under that?', going deeper and deeper and deeper, to the point where you really get to the hub of it. Because then you can look at it, then you can face it. And we can face anything. But we have to get there.

The Crown Chakra reminds us that while we are unique individuals, we are also part of something infinitely larger—

whether you conceptualise that as the universe, nature, collective consciousness, divine presence, or simply the vast web of life that connects all beings.

## "I Am Not My Mother": The Paradox of Resistance

Many of us reach a point in life where we look at patterns in our family and declare, often with fierce determination, "I will not be like that. I will not repeat those mistakes."

Perhaps you've said it yourself: "I will never speak to my children the way I was spoken to." "I will never be as disorganised/ rigid/emotional/detached as my mother." "I will create a completely different kind of relationship than my parents had."

These declarations come from a genuine desire for growth and healing. But there's a fascinating paradox at work here: what we resist often persists, sometimes in surprising ways.

"Hannah" came to me deeply frustrated. "I've spent my whole life determined not to become my mother," she told me. "She was always putting everyone else's needs before her own, never setting boundaries, always exhausted. I swore I'd be different—and yet here I am, burning out from overgiving, just like she did."

What Hannah was experiencing wasn't failure—it was a profound invitation to go beyond simple resistance to true transformation. Because here's the truth: simply trying not to be something keeps us energetically bound to it. It's like trying not to think of a pink elephant—the very act of resistance keeps the image front and centre in our minds. We have to.

True freedom comes not from battling against what we don't want to become, but from embracing what we don't want to even entertain in Hannah's case "I'm just like my mother" for example and then consciously creating what we do want to embody. It's the difference between moving away from something versus moving toward something else entirely.

As Hannah and I worked together, she began to shift her focus from "not being like my mother" to "creating my own relationship with giving and receiving." This subtle but profound shift moved her from resistance to creation, from reaction to conscious choice.

The patterns we inherit are neither curses to battle nor destinies we must fulfil—they are simply starting points from which we can consciously evolve.

## The Mirror Effect:
## What Others Reflect Back

Have you noticed how certain people in your life seem perfectly designed to trigger your deepest insecurities or unhealed wounds? This isn't a coincidence (actually I don't believe in coincidence!) —it's what I call the Mirror Effect, and it's one of the most powerful teachers on our path to wholeness.

The people who challenge us most are often reflecting aspects of ourselves that we haven't fully acknowledged, accepted, or integrated. This doesn't mean we are exactly like them—rather, they're highlighting areas within us that still need attention and healing.

Think about someone who really triggers you. Perhaps it's a family member whose neediness exhausts you. Maybe it's a colleague whose arrogance grates on your nerves. Or possibly a friend whose people-pleasing frustrates you.

Now, ask yourself: What might this person be mirroring back to me? Is there a part of me—perhaps one I don't readily acknowledge—that shares this quality? Or is this quality triggering me because it reflects a wound I haven't fully healed?

I remember working with a client—let's call her Julie—who was consistently frustrated by her partner's insecurity and need for reassurance. 'Why can't he just know that I love him?' she would ask, exasperated. 'Why does he need me to say it all the time?'

As we explored this trigger more deeply, Julie realised something surprising: her partner's open vulnerability around needing love was activating her own unacknowledged fears of not being enough, fears she'd spent a lifetime burying beneath a confident exterior. His willingness to ask for what he needed highlighted her inability to do the same.

This recognition didn't immediately solve their dynamic, but it shifted something crucial—Julie began to see her irritation not as evidence of her partner's problem, but as a signpost pointing toward her own healing journey.

This is how the Crown Chakra wisdom works in our everyday lives. It helps us rise above our immediate reactions to see the larger patterns at play, to recognise that our relationships are constantly offering us opportunities for growth and greater wholeness.

## The Crown Chakra: Your Connection to Something Greater

The ancient teachers called this energy centre 'Sahasrara'—which means "thousand-petaled lotus." This beautiful image captures something essential about this chakra: it opens us to infinite possibilities beyond our limited perspective, just as a lotus with a thousand petals opens to the vastness of the sky.

**In our everyday lives, the Crown Chakra is where:**

- Personal will meets higher purpose
- Individual identity opens to universal connection
- Limited thinking expands into broader awareness
- Control softens into trust
- Separation dissolves into oneness

**When this energy centre is flowing freely, you might notice:**

- Synchronicities that seem to guide your path
- A sense of being part of something larger than yourself
- Inspiration that seems to arrive from beyond your thinking mind
- Deep trust in life's unfolding, even during challenges
- A natural sense of gratitude and wonder

**But when it's blocked (as is common in our individualistic culture), you might find:**

- Feeling isolated and solely responsible for everything
- Excessive focus on material achievement without deeper fulfilment

- Spiritual emptiness or disconnection
- Rigid thinking and the need to control outcomes
- Difficulty surrendering to life's natural flow

The Crown Chakra doesn't ask us to abandon our individuality or practical concerns—rather, it invites us to hold them within a larger context of meaning and connection. Like a bird that needs both wings to fly, we need both earthly engagement and spiritual awareness to live our fullest lives.

## Nature versus Nurture: The Dance of Soul and Conditioning

We often speak of "nature versus nurture" when discussing what shapes us. But perhaps it's more accurate to think of "nature and nurture"—an ongoing dance between our essential nature (who we truly are at soul level) and our nurture (the conditioning we've received).

**Think of it this way:**

- Your nature is like the seed—with its unique potential and inherent qualities
- Your nurture is like the soil, water, and light—shaping how that seed grows
- Both are essential, both are powerful, and both deserve acknowledgment.

I've noticed in my work that many of our deepest struggles emerge from conflicts between our authentic nature and our conditioning. When what we've been taught contradicts what we know in our bones to be true for us, we experience inner division and confusion.

**Some common examples include:**

- Being naturally expressive but raised in a family that valued stoicism
- Having artistic talents but conditioned to pursue only "practical" paths
- Being naturally intuitive but taught to trust only logical thinking
- Having a contemplative temperament but raised to value constant activity
- Being naturally generous but conditioned to fear scarcity

When we can't distinguish between our authentic nature and our conditioning, we often live lives that feel somehow "off"—as if we're trying to be someone we're not, or living according to a script that doesn't fit our true essence.

The Crown Chakra helps us rise above both nature and nurture to see them clearly, to distinguish between them, and to consciously choose which conditioning serves our authentic nature and which we're ready to release.

## Balance of Structure and Surrender: The Ellev8 Way

Just as we've explored in previous chapters, the wisdom of the Crown Chakra emerges through balancing complementary energies—what we might call the masculine and feminine aspects of spiritual connection.

This balance is at the heart of the Ellev8 philosophy:

The masculine energy gives us focus, dedication, and the structures through which purpose manifests. The feminine energy gives us receptivity, intuition, and the ability to surrender to something greater than our personal will. Neither is complete without the other. Together, they create a spirituality that is both grounded and transcendent, both active and receptive.

**Think about these complementary approaches to purpose:**

- Structure without surrender can become rigid, missing the flow of divine timing
- Surrender without structure can become passive, lacking the focused action that brings vision into reality

I worked with a client— "Sophia"—who came to me feeling deeply frustrated with her spiritual path. "I've been meditating for years," she told me. "I've attended retreats, read countless books, done all the 'right' practices. But I still feel disconnected from any real sense of purpose."

As we worked together, a pattern emerged: Sophia had been approaching spirituality primarily through structured practices and mental understanding. What was missing was the feminine aspect of surrender—the willingness to open to mystery, to receive guidance rather than achieving enlightenment, to allow purpose to find her rather than hunting it down.

As she began to balance her structured practices with more receptive ones—silent walking in nature, freeform journaling, periods of simply being without agenda—something shifted. Purpose began to reveal itself not as a dramatic calling, but as a gentle unfolding of meaning in everyday moments.

This is the dance of Crown Chakra wisdom—holding the tension between dedicated practice and open surrender, between focused intention and receptive allowing. Neither alone creates the fullest expression of our spiritual nature; together, they open us to both depth and height.

## Breaking the Patterns: From Recognition to Freedom

Understanding the patterns we've inherited is just the beginning. The real transformation happens when we move from recognition to conscious choice—when we can see our conditioning clearly and decide what to keep, what to release, and what to transform.

**Here's a gentle process I've found helpful in working with inherited patterns:**

**Recognition:** Notice a pattern without judgment. "I see that I approach conflict the same way my father did" or "I notice I have the same beliefs about money that dominated my family."

**Compassionate Understanding:** Explore why this pattern developed. Often, what we inherit served a purpose in its original context, even if it no longer serves us. "This pattern helped my family survive difficult economic circumstances" or "This approach to emotions made sense in the environment my parents grew up in."

**Discernment:** Decide what aspects of this pattern still serve you and which don't. Not everything inherited needs to be rejected—some patterns carry deep wisdom.

**Conscious Choice:** Actively choose how you want to relate to this aspect of life. Not just moving away from the old pattern, but moving toward a new expression that feels authentically yours.

**Practice and Patience:** Recognize that transforming deep patterns takes time. Old neural pathways don't disappear overnight, but with consistent new choices, new pathways form.

This process isn't about rejecting your lineage or judging those who came before you. It's about honouring their journey while claiming your right to continue evolving. As the poet David Whyte beautifully puts it: *"You are not a troubled guest on this earth, you are not an accident amidst other accidents, you were invited from another and greater night than the one from which you have just emerged."*

# Practical Ways to Strengthen Your Crown Chakra

Just as we've explored practical ways to work with each chakra, here are some gentle approaches to strengthen your connection with the Crown Chakra. These aren't complicated techniques—they're simple practices that create space for deeper awareness:

### ◯ The Surrender Practice

This is beautiful to do with your morning tea or coffee. Take a moment to identify something you've been trying to control or figure out through sheer mental effort. As you hold your warm cup, say quietly: "I release my need to control this. I open to guidance beyond my thinking mind." Feel the subtle shift from grasping to allowing.

### The Wisdom Walk

This simple practice helps you access wisdom beyond your analytical mind. Take a walk in nature without a specific destination. As you walk, hold a question that's important to you—not analyzing it, just carrying it gently. Notice what arises: images, feelings, overheard conversations, or natural symbols that seem to speak to your question. The answers often come not in words, but in subtle knowing that emerges when the thinking mind relaxes.

### The Lineage Meditation

This powerful practice helps you see your place in the larger flow of generations. Sit quietly and visualize behind you the long line of your ancestors—known and unknown—stretching back through time. Feel their presence, their gifts, their challenges that have shaped you. Then visualize before you the generations that will follow, whether your direct descendants or those your life will touch in some way. Feel yourself as the bridge between past and future, honouring what came before while consciously choosing what you pass forward.

When you're feeling particularly disconnected or overwhelmed by life's challenges, try this:

**The Crown Connection:**
- Find a quiet space where you won't be disturbed
- Sit comfortably and take several deep breaths
- Gently rest your hands on your lap, palms open upward
- Imagine a soft light at the crown of your head
- With each breath, allow that light to expand

- Feel yourself opening to guidance and support beyond your personal resources
- Simply receive whatever comes—insights, feelings, images, or simply peace
- Close by thanking this larger wisdom, however you conceptualize it

This isn't about perfecting a technique—it's about creating space for connection to something beyond yourself, whatever name or form that takes for you.

# Taking a Deeper Look

As in previous chapters, I invite you to sit with these questions—not to find immediate answers, but to create space for deeper understanding to emerge:

**Think about...**

1. What family patterns have you inherited that you're now ready to examine with compassion? These might be obvious patterns or subtle ones that only reveal themselves in certain situations.

2. Who in your life triggers strong reactions in you, and what might they be mirroring back? Remember, strong reactions often point to unintegrated aspects of ourselves.

3. Where do you tend to over-control, and what might happen if you surrendered more to life's flow? Control often masks deeper fears that need gentle exploration.

4. How do you conceptualize that which is greater than yourself? Whether you relate to this as God, Universe, Higher Self, Nature, or simply Mystery, how do you experience this connection?

5. What inherited beliefs about spirituality shape your current relationship with the transcendent? Many of us carry early religious or spiritual conditioning that benefits from conscious examination.

6. In what areas of life do you feel most guided or supported by something beyond your personal will? These

experiences offer clues to strengthening your Crown Chakra connection.

7. Where do you sense a conflict between your authentic nature and your conditioning? These friction points often indicate where healing and integration are needed.

8. What would become possible if you fully trusted the unfolding of your life? This isn't about passivity, but about aligning your will with a larger wisdom.

As with all our reflections, let these questions simmer gently. Notice what emerges in quiet moments, perhaps when you're at your window watching the sky change, or when you're engaged in simple daily rituals.

Use this space to jot down anything that comes up for you.

# Coming Home to Something Greater

You know in the evening when I open my window to the night sky? There's something about gazing into that vast expanse of stars that puts everything into perspective. My daily concerns—so consuming in the moment—suddenly find their proper scale against the backdrop of infinite space and time.

This is what Crown Chakra awareness offers us—not an escape from our humanness, but a larger context for it. A recognition that while our individual journey matters deeply, it unfolds within something infinitely greater than our personal storyline.

Developing this connection isn't about achieving some perfect spiritual state. It's more like my morning and evening window practices—something we return to, day after day. Sometimes we feel profound connection. Other times we mainly notice our disconnection. Both experiences are part of the path.

**Remember:**

- Your patterns and conditioning aren't your destiny—they're just your starting point
- What triggers you in others often reveals what needs healing within
- True freedom comes not from controlling life but from dancing with it
- You are both a unique individual AND part of something infinitely larger

Before we move on to the final chapter, I invite you to choose one small way to connect with something greater today. Perhaps it's pausing to feel gratitude for the intricate web of life that sustains you. Maybe it's opening to guidance about a challenge you've been trying to solve alone. Or simply taking a moment to gaze at the sky and remember your place in this vast, mysterious universe.

What matters isn't how dramatic your practice is—it's the sincerity with which you open to something beyond your individual self.

Are you ready to explore what comes next in our final chapter?

# Recipe:
# Royal Moroccan Orange Salad

This beautiful and delicious desert is fit for any Queen, Empress or crowned being…. (that's you…)

This #Ellev8's oranges to a whole new level and makes a regal ending to any meal.

## Ingredients for 2

- 1 large orange
- Rosewater
- Olive oil
- Sea salt crystals
- A few pink peppercorns, crushed
- ¼ teaspoon ground cinnamon

## The Practice

1. Peel the orange so it is completely clear of pith
2. Slice thinly but thick enough to hold in one piece when lifted. Arrange on a platter with slightly upturned edges.
3. Put your thumb over the top of the bottle and drizzle with olive oil, do the same with rosewater.
4. Sprinkle with cinnamon, sprinkle with salt crystals and peppercorns

It's important to use salt crystals not ground sea salt - you want the "pop" of a salt "hit" not a salted salad.

This is so easy but so special

## Chapter 8
# INTEGRATION
*Bringing It All Together*

---
*"You are the creator of your own story. The question is—how will you write your next chapter?"*

---

### Dear Ellev8'ing One,

Have you ever noticed how the most profound insights often arrive in the most ordinary moments? Perhaps while making your morning tea, watching rain trace patterns on your window, or folding laundry still warm from the dryer. It's rarely when we're striving for transformation that it finds us—it's in those quiet moments of presence when something within us quietly shifts.

I was sitting in my garden at dusk yesterday, watching bees make their final visits to the heather. As the day's light softened into evening, I found myself reflecting on our journey together through these pages. Step by step, chakra by chakra, we've explored what it means to live with greater awareness, authenticity, and alignment.

But here's the truth that I've learned over years of working with people on their transformation journeys: knowing about these principles is just the beginning. The real magic happens when we bring this awareness into our everyday lives—not as something separate from our ordinary routines, but woven into the very fabric of how we move through each day.

This final chapter isn't about adding more knowledge. It's about integration—taking everything we've explored together and finding simple, sustainable ways to embody it. Not in dramatic gestures or perfect practices, but in the thousand small choices we make each day that, over time, completely reshape our experience of life.

### With love, light and grace
### Karen 🩶 xxx

# From Learning to Living: The Journey of Integration

**Throughout this book, we've been on a journey through the seven energy centres, starting from the ground and moving upward:**

- 🌱 **The Root Chakra (Chapter 1)** – Where we found our foundation, transforming fear into trust and security
- 💧 **The Sacral Chakra (Chapter 2)** – Where we reclaimed our creative flow, pleasure, and natural rhythms
- ◯ **The Solar Plexus Chakra (Chapter 3)** – Where we stepped into our personal power and authentic confidence
- 💚 **The Heart Chakra (Chapter 4)** – Where we opened to deeper connection, compassion, and love
- 🎤 **The Throat Chakra (Chapter 5)** – Where we found our voice and learned to express our truth
- 👁 **The Third Eye Chakra (Chapter 6)** – Where we developed our inner vision and intuitive wisdom
- ◯ **The Crown Chakra (Chapter 7)** – Where we connected to something greater than ourselves

Each of these centres has offered its own wisdom, its own healing, its own invitation to live more fully. But the real question now is: How do we bring all of this together? How do we live from this integrated awareness, not just in special moments of practice or insight, but in the messiness and beauty of everyday life?

This is where true transformation happens—not in the spiritual highs or the perfect practices, but in how we show up on ordinary Tuesday afternoons when we're tired, when the car needs repair, when someone we love is struggling, when life is simply being life in all its complexity.

Integration isn't about perfection. It's about presence. It's about bringing consciousness to parts of our lives that have been running on autopilot. It's about making choices that align with our deepest values, even when those choices are challenging. And perhaps most importantly, it's about gentleness—meeting ourselves with compassion as we navigate this human journey.

## The Ellev8 Infinity Flow: The Dance of Energies

Throughout this book, we've explored the Ellev8 philosophy through the infinity symbol (∞) and what it represents—the continuous flow between complementary energies. This symbol reminds us that life isn't static; it's a constant dance between different ways of being and doing.

Think of it as the breath of life itself—the natural rhythm of expansion and contraction, giving and receiving, structure and flow. Just as we can't only inhale or only exhale, we can't fully thrive by expressing only one type of energy.

**The Ellev8 approach invites us to embrace both:**

**Yin Energy (Feminine):**

- Receptive, intuitive, feeling, allowing
- Presence, embodiment, connection, nurturing
- Flow, creativity, surrender, trust

**Yang Energy (Masculine):**

- Active, focused, structured, directed
- Boundaries, clarity, decisiveness, protection
- Action, manifestation, purpose, forward momentum

Integration isn't about perfectly balancing these energies at all times—that would be exhausting and unnatural. Rather, it's about developing the awareness and flexibility to move between them as each situation calls for. It's about knowing when to act and when to allow, when to speak and when to listen, when to lead and when to follow.

"Rachel" came to me feeling completely burnt out. She was a highly successful business strategist, brilliant at the masculine energy of action, structure, and achievement. But she had almost completely neglected the feminine energies of receptivity, rest, and flow.

"I feel like I'm always pushing," she told me. "Even my relaxation is scheduled and optimised!"

As we worked together, Rachel began to recognise that her depletion wasn't from working too hard—it was from operating almost exclusively in one energy. She wasn't allowing herself to receive, to be nourished, to flow with life rather than always directing it.

Her integration journey wasn't about abandoning her powerful capacity for focused action. It was about complementing it with periods of genuine receptivity—learning to listen to her body's wisdom, to trust that not everything needed to be forced, to allow support and nourishment to flow into her life.

Within months, not only did her energy and wellbeing dramatically improve, but her work became more inspired and effective. By integrating both energies, she found a sustainable rhythm that allowed her to thrive rather than merely survive.

This is the essence of the Ellev8 approach—not choosing between different energies, but learning to dance with them all, allowing each to inform and strengthen the others.

## Signs of True Integration: Recognising Your Progress

The **Ellev8 Leader** is someone who doesn't just *understand* transformation—they *embody* it.

How do you know if you're truly integrating these principles into your life? It's rarely a dramatic moment of arrival—more often, it's subtle shifts that you might only notice when you pause to reflect.

**Here are some quiet signs that integration is happening:**

- You feel less fragmented. Rather than different aspects of your life feeling disconnected (work self, home self, social self), there's a growing sense of coherence. You're bringing your whole self to each situation, even as you adapt to different contexts.
- Decisions become clearer. Not because you always know the "right" answer immediately, but because you trust your process of discernment. You can feel when something aligns with your truest self and when it doesn't.
- You recover more quickly. Challenges still arise (they always will), but you find yourself bouncing back more readily,

without getting stuck in old patterns of reaction or shutdown.
- Your relationships deepen. As you become more integrated within yourself, your connections with others naturally become more authentic. There's less performing, less hiding, more genuine presence.
- You trust life's timing. There's less pushing against what is and more dancing with it. You recognise when to take action and when to allow things to unfold in their own time.
- You feel more at home in your body. Integration isn't just a mental or spiritual process—it happens in the body too. You might notice more ease, more embodied presence, a greater sense of being at home in your physical self.
- You laugh more easily. Perhaps especially at yourself! There's a lightness that comes with integration, an ability to hold life less tightly, to see the humour in the human journey.

Remember, integration is not a destination but an ongoing process. There will always be areas where we're more integrated than others, always edges of growth and discovery. The key is to meet yourself wherever you are with kindness and curiosity, celebrating progress without demanding perfection.

# The Wheel of Life: Checking Your Vitals

Just as we began this book by checking in with ourselves, let's take a moment to assess where you are now across the different areas of your life. This isn't about scoring yourself or finding fault—it's about honest awareness, the starting point for any meaningful integration.

**Take a moment to reflect on each area below, noticing both your current experience and where you might want to direct more conscious attention:**

1. **Work & Purpose**

Structure: Do you have clarity about your direction and boundaries in your work?
Flow: Does your work feel fulfilling, aligned with your values and natural gifts?

2. **Family & Relationships**

Structure: Are you showing up consistently and with clear communication?
Flow: Are your connections nurturing, authentic, and emotionally rich?

3. **Financial Wellbeing**

Structure: Are you managing resources wisely with appropriate planning?
Flow: Do you have a healthy relationship with giving and receiving?

4. **Spiritual Connection**

Structure: Do you have regular practices that support your spiritual growth?
Flow: Do you feel a genuine connection to something larger than yourself?

5. **Health & Vitality**

Structure: Are you supporting your body with movement, nutrition, and rest?
Flow: Are you listening to your body's wisdom and natural rhythms?

6. **Play & Joy**

Structure: Do you make space for activities that bring genuine delight?
Flow: Can you access spontaneity, curiosity, and lightness of being?

7. **Contribution & Leadership**

Structure: Are you using your gifts in service to something meaningful?
Flow: Does your contribution emerge naturally from your authentic self?

8. **Personal Growth**

Structure: Are you committed to ongoing learning and development?
Flow: Are you gentle with yourself in the process, allowing growth to unfold naturally?

As you reflect on these areas, notice where you feel most aligned and where you sense opportunities for greater integration. The aim isn't balance in the sense of giving equal attention to everything at once—that's neither realistic nor desirable. Life moves in seasons, and different areas naturally come into focus at different times.

What matters is conscious choice—being intentional about where you direct your energy based on your values and current needs, rather than operating on autopilot or external expectations.

# Bringing It All Together: Daily Practices for Integration

Integration happens in the small moments of everyday life, not just in dedicated practice time. Here are some simple ways to bring what you've learned into your daily experience:

### The Morning Alignment Practice

Before checking your phone or getting caught in the day's demands, take a few moments to set your internal compass:

- Feel your feet on the floor, establishing your grounding (Root Chakra)
- Take three deep breaths into your belly, connecting with your life force (Sacral Chakra)
- Place a hand on your solar plexus, feeling your personal power (Solar Plexus Chakra)
- Rest your other hand on your heart, awakening compassion (Heart Chakra)
- Touch your throat gently, honouring your voice (Throat Chakra)
- Bring attention to the space between your eyebrows, inviting clarity (Third Eye Chakra)
- Imagine a soft light at the crown of your head, connecting to guidance (Crown Chakra)
- Ask yourself: "What quality do I most need to embody today?"

This entire practice can take less than two minutes, yet it creates a powerful foundation for your day.

### 🌿 The Energy Check-In

Throughout your day, particularly before important interactions or decisions, take a moment to check your energy:

- Pause and take a conscious breath
- Notice: Am I in pushing energy or allowing energy right now?
- Ask: What's actually needed in this situation?
- Adjust your approach accordingly

This simple check-in helps you move beyond habitual reactions to conscious responses, allowing you to bring the most appropriate energy to each situation.

### 🌙 The Evening Integration

As your day comes to a close, perhaps while sipping evening tea or preparing for sleep:

- Reflect on moments when you felt aligned and integrated
- List everything you are grateful for, specifically from today
- Acknowledge moments when you felt disconnected or out of balance
- Rather than judging yourself, simply notice what you can learn
- Set a gentle intention for how you'd like to approach tomorrow

This reflection isn't about critique—it's about learning and integration. What patterns do you notice? What small adjustments might support greater alignment?

### The Pattern Interrupt

When you notice yourself falling into old patterns that don't serve you:

- Pause and take a conscious breath
- Place a hand on your heart
- Ask: "What would my wisest self do right now?"
- Listen for the answer that comes from your deeper wisdom, not your reactive patterns

This simple practice creates space between trigger and response, allowing you to choose your action rather than being driven by unconscious patterns.

Remember, integration isn't about perfection or following an exact formula. It's about bringing consciousness to how you move through your days, making choices that align with your deepest values rather than being pulled along by habit or external pressure.

As with any practice, the key is consistency rather than intensity. Small, sustainable shifts create far more lasting transformation than dramatic changes that quickly burn out.

# Taking a Deeper Look: Questions for Integration

As we've done throughout our journey together, let's pause for reflection. These questions invite you to explore your relationship with integration more deeply:

**Think about...**

1. Which chakra or energy centre do you feel most naturally aligned with? We all have areas where integration comes more easily. Recognising your natural strengths provides a foundation to build from.

2. Which chakra feels most challenging for you right now? Areas of challenge often hold the greatest opportunities for growth and integration.

3. What daily habit or practice has been most supportive for your wellbeing? Sometimes the simplest practices create the most profound shifts.

4. Where do you tend to abandon yourself when under pressure? Many of us have habitual ways we disconnect from our deeper wisdom when stressed or challenged.

5. What would become possible if you fully trusted the unfolding of your life? Integration often involves releasing the illusion of control while remaining fully engaged.

6. How has your relationship with masculine and feminine energies evolved? Notice if you're more comfortable with one energy and how you might create greater balance.

7. What one small adjustment could create greater alignment in your daily life? Integration happens through small, consistent shifts rather than dramatic overhauls.

8. How would you like to feel one year from now? Setting an intention based on feeling rather than specific achievements often leads to more authentic outcomes.

As always, approach these questions with gentle curiosity rather than seeking "correct" answers. Let them simmer in your awareness over the coming days, noticing what emerges in quiet moments.

Use this space to jot down anything that comes up for you.

# Recipe:
# Ellev8'ed Brussel Sprout Salad

Brussel sprouts are something of a "marmite" ingredient but trust me on this you've never had them like this! Integrated with dates, Parmesan cheese, sage and balsamic vinegar they go to another level.

## Ingredients, for 2

- 125g (4½oz) brussel sprouts, finely sliced
- 2 Medjool dates, stones removed and finely chopped
- 2 tablespoons Parmesan (Parmigiano) cheese, finely grated
- 1 teaspoon dried sage (dried is actually better than fresh in this, fresh is a bit too pungent)
- 1 tablespoon balsamic vinegar
- Sea salt & cracked black pepper (you may not need salt)

## The Practice

Mix all together and adjust quantities to suit your taste - more sweet, more salty, more sharp

If this doesn't show the benefits of integration I don't know what does! It truly Ellev8's all the ingredients to another level.

# Your Next Chapter: Writing Your Own Story

You know in the evenings when I open my window to the night sky? There's something about that moment that always reminds me of an essential truth: we are both infinitely small in the grand cosmic perspective and incredibly significant in our capacity to choose, to create, to love, to grow.

This paradox is at the heart of an integrated life—holding both our humility and our power, both our limitations and our boundless potential. It's about recognising that while we don't control everything that happens to us, we always have choice in how we respond, in what meaning we make, in how we show up.

As we come to the end of our journey together through these pages, I invite you to recognise that your life's next chapter belongs to you. Not in the sense of controlling every outcome, but in the profound truth that you get to choose how you meet each moment, how you embody your values, how you express your unique gifts.

Integration isn't a final destination—it's an ongoing dance with life. There will always be new insights to incorporate, new edges of growth to explore, new depths of wisdom to embody. That's not a failure of integration; it's the beautiful nature of being human.

**Remember:**

- Integration happens in ordinary moments, not just peak experiences

- The dance between different energies is natural and necessary
- Small, consistent shifts create more lasting change than dramatic overhauls
- Compassion for yourself in the process is essential, not optional

Before we part, I invite you to take a moment to acknowledge how far you've come—not just through reading this book, but through your entire journey of growth and awakening. Each insight you've gained, each pattern you've recognised, each moment of greater awareness—these are all sacred steps on your path.

The word "integration" comes from the Latin "integrare," meaning "to make whole." That's my deepest wish for you—not perfection, but wholeness. Not a life without challenges, but a life where every experience, every emotion, every aspect of yourself is welcomed into the embrace of your awareness.

You are the author of your next chapter. How will you choose to write it?

The key thing here is, if you're reading this, you're ready. And I am so, so pleased you are. Because the world needs you. It needs you in all your glory, all your light, all your love, shining bright. Because we need it. The world needs it. I need it. You need it. We all need it.

We are incredibly powerful. And that's exciting. It's scary too, because, yes, they are two sides of the same coin: scary, exciting. And then eventually you get to a place of being at one with what is, <u>really</u> being at one with what is. You actually get to a point where nothing is scary or exciting. It just is.

We have time. It's about choices. It's about priorities. And anyway, we can bend time. It's an illusion. When you start getting into meditation, you really see how you can bend time. We can do it all. We are so much more powerful than we give ourselves credit for.

With love for your journey,
Karen ♥ xxx

# NEXT STEPS FOR YOU THE READER

***Dear Ellev8'ing One,***

As our journey through these pages comes to a close, I'd like to share some thoughts about how to keep this work alive in your life. Transformation isn't a destination we reach once and then reside in forever—it's a path we walk daily, moment by moment, choice by choice.

Here are some gentle invitations for continuing your journey:

## Keep the Practice Alive

This book isn't meant to sit on a shelf gathering dust once read. Its true value emerges when you return to it again and again, letting different sections speak to you as you need them.

- Revisit chapters when you feel stuck or sense a particular chakra needs attention.
- Use the reflection questions regularly as journaling prompts or meditation focuses.
- Integrate the rituals and practices into your daily rhythm in ways that feel natural to you.

Make sure you've downloaded your copy of the companion Workbook to Ellev8 Book One "Letting the Light in". It is for sale on Amazon and elsewhere but... as a Gift to enhance your whole experience as you go on this journey with me I would like to give you a copy of the pdf

You can download it via the QR code or at this link:

https://tinyurl.com/Letting-the-Light-in-Workbook

Remember the simplest practices are often the most powerful. You don't need elaborate rituals or perfect conditions to continue this work. A conscious breath while waiting for the kettle to boil, a moment of grounding while standing in a queue, or a pause to check in with your intuition before making a decision—these small moments of awareness create profound shifts over time.

## Share Your Insights

Growth deepens when shared. Not only does articulating your insights help integrate them more fully, but sharing your journey may offer others exactly what they need at the perfect moment.

- Discuss what you've learned with trusted friends or in circles where vulnerability is honoured.
- Write about your experiences—perhaps in a private journal, in letters to yourself, or in more public formats if that feels aligned. (email me personally: karen@karenkennaby.com, I'd love to hear from you)

✳ If this book has supported your journey, consider sharing it with someone who might benefit from these same perspectives.

Please leave a review on Amazon. A short honest review would mean the world to me, reviews are the lifeblood of any author and help make sure the book gets into the right hands. Thank you so much

Remember that sharing isn't about having all the answers or presenting a perfect transformation. It's about authentic connection around our shared human experience of growth, challenge, and awakening.

## Connect with Ellev8

Ellev8 is more than just a concept or a book—it's a community of like-minded souls walking this path of balanced transformation together.

- ✳ [Join the Ellev8 community](#) to connect with others on similar journeys.
- ✳ Listen to the "Around the Table with Karen" or Ellev8 podcast for deeper explorations of these themes.
- ✳ Visit [Ellev8.World] for resources, courses, and events designed to support your continued growth.

There's profound power in finding others who speak the same language of transformation, who understand both the challenges and the joys of this path. In fact I was talking about this just today over lunch with a friend who is moving a long way away, and she was wondering where she would find her new community. We aren't meant to walk alone—we're designed for connection and mutual support.

## Step Fully into Your Power

You are no longer quite the same person who began reading these pages. Whether the shifts have been subtle or dramatic, something has changed. New awareness has dawned, new possibilities have opened.

Now comes the beautiful, challenging invitation: to step forward into your life with this expanded consciousness, to integrate your insights not just in special moments of practice but in how you move through each ordinary day.

Remember that your power isn't about perfection—it's about presence. It's about bringing consciousness to choices that may have once been automatic. It's about recognising when old patterns arise and gently choosing a new response. It's about coming home to yourself, again and again.

## Closing Statement

"There is no final destination, only deeper layers of becoming."

You've journeyed through eight aspects of transformation, exploring the wisdom of each chakra—from the grounding security of your foundation to the expansive connection of your spiritual centre. You've peeled back layers of conditioning, illuminated fears that may have limited you, and reconnected with aspects of yourself that may have been buried beneath expected roles and identities.

But this isn't an ending—it's a threshold.

Transformation isn't a one-time event; it's a way of living. It's how we meet each moment with greater awareness, greater compassion, greater authenticity.

**Every day invites you to:**

- Choose trust over fear, even when uncertainty arises
- Speak your truth with both courage and kindness
- Honour both your need for structure and your capacity for flow
- Lead with an open heart while standing firmly in your power

The path ahead belongs to you. Not in the sense of controlling every outcome (life will always bring its surprises), but in consciously choosing how you meet what comes, what meaning you make of it, and how you allow it to shape you.

You are not defined by your past, though it has offered invaluable lessons. You are not limited by others' expectations, though they may have influenced you. You are not bound by fears, though they may have once protected you.

You are something new. You are becoming more fully yourself with every conscious choice, every moment of presence, every act of courage or compassion.

This is your life. This is your story. This is your time.

# Final Words:
# Stay Open, Stay Curious, Stay Brave

The journey doesn't end here. In fact, the more you grow, the deeper the invitation becomes. Each layer of awareness reveals new dimensions to explore, new edges to expand, new depths to embody.

- 💜 When clarity seems elusive, return to the quiet knowing within you.
- 💜 When fear arises, come back to your breath, your body, your grounding.
- 💜 When resistance appears, approach it with curiosity—it often guards important wisdom.

You are not alone on this path. You are connected to something larger than yourself—whether you conceptualise that as nature, the universe, divine presence, or simply the vast web of life that holds us all. This larger wisdom supports you, guides you, and often speaks through your own deepest intuition.

The universe isn't simply happening to you—it's happening with you and through you. Your consciousness, your choices, your presence matters. The world needs your particular light, your unique gifts, your authentic voice.

Thank you for walking this path, for doing this inner work, for being willing to grow. It matters more than you know—not just for your own life, but for all the lives you touch, directly and indirectly.

Now, go live it. Not perfectly, but presently. Not without challenges, but with growing wisdom to meet them. Not alone, but connected to both your own deep resources and the larger web of support that surrounds you.

The light within me honours the light within you.

*With love, light and grace,*
*Karen* 🩶 *xxx*

PS This is not an isolated book - it became clear very quickly once I started work on it that it is, in fact, Book One of Eight...so when you've finished this one look out for Book Two!

PPS and if you haven't yet downloaded your Gift copy of the companion workbook you can do so here via the QR code or at link: https://tinyurl.com/Letting-the-Light-in-Workbook

PPPS **please** leave a review on Amazon! A short honest review would mean the world to me, reviews are the lifeblood of any author and help make sure the book gets into the right hands. Thank you so much xxx

# ABOUT THE AUTHOR

Karen Kennaby Founder Ellev8; Curator of Exquisite Journeys and Catalyst for Transformation

Karen Kennaby, founded and ran, for 21 years, a 7-figure event management business with a team of 24; has run several membership organisations, in both the UK and the Middle East, and has been a successful coach/mentor to women around the globe for over two decades. She also loves hosting and facilitating events globally both live and online.

Karen helps women 45+ answer those big – "shall I stay or shall I go" questions in life around work, home, relationships. Clients are often at a major crossroads and needing to make a big decision. Sometimes described as a "Warrior Queen" Karen is able to see the potential for her clients when they can't and with her decades of business and entrepreneurial experience she is able to guide them through the vision creation, plan development and implementation to generate success in their own unique way and she does so with love, compassion and understanding.

Client testimonials often allude to the magical quality of her work:

"She's an amazing woman who I occasionally described as 'scary' because she often knew me better than I knew myself!"

Another says:

"You are absolutely unique, pure magic. In 45 minutes you managed to give me all the answers I needed"

Karen is able to see the bigger picture and her passion lies in helping women create more joyful lives whilst creating major impact in their own lives and the lives of others.

This passion led Karen to create Ellev8 – a global movement attracting women who want to create a legacy with real social impact. Ellev8 incorporates Karen's unique style of coaching/mentoring both 1:1 and in small groups, retreats alongside her Unique & Exquisite Journeys and signature Around The Table With Karen.

Printed in Dunstable, United Kingdom